Also by Dave Barry

The Taming of the Shrew
Babies and Other Hazards of Sex
Stay Fit and Healthy Until You're Dead
Claw Your Way to the Top
Bad Habits
Dave Barry's Guide to Marriage and/or Sex
Homes and Other Black Holes
Dave Barry's Greatest Hits
Dave Barry Slept Here
Dave Barry Turns 40
Dave Barry Talks Back
Dave Barry's Only Travel Guide You'll Ever Need
Dave Barry Does Japan
Dave Barry is Not *Making This Up*
Dave Barry's Gift Guide to End All Gift Guides
Dave Barry's Complete Guide to Guys
Dave Barry in Cyberspace
Dave Barry's Book of Bad Songs
Dave Barry Is from Mars and *Venus*
Big Trouble
Dave Barry Is Not Taking This Sitting Down
Dave Barry Hits Below the Beltway
Tricky Business

DAVE BARRY Turns 50

The Random House Publishing Group
New York

A Ballantine Book
Published by The Random House Publishing Group

Copyright © 1998 by Dave Barry

Published in the United States by Ballantine Books, an imprint of The Random House Publishing Group, a division of Random House, Inc., New York, and simultaneously in Canada by Random House of Canada, Ltd., Toronto.

Ballantine and colophon are registered trademarks of Random House, Inc.

www.ballantinebooks.com

Library of Congress Catalog Card Number: 99-90674

ISBN: 0-345-43169-3

This edition published by arrangement with Crown Publishers, Inc.

Cover photo by Bill Wax

Manufactured in the United States of America

First Ballantine Books Edition: September 1999

19 18 17 16 15 14 13 12

CONTENTS

DAVE BARRY

Turns

50

1

It's Great to Be 50!

Right. And Herbert Hoover was a rap singer.

I am NOT going to whine.

Yes, I have turned 50.

Yes, this is an age that I used to consider old. Not middle-aged, like Dick Van Dyke and Mary Tyler Moore in *The Dick Van Dyke Show;* but actually *old*, like Walter Brennan as Granpappy Amos in *The Real McCoys*, gimping around cluelessly in a pair of bib overalls and saying things like "Con-SARN it!"

But I do not choose to dwell on the negative. I choose to be an optimist, like the great explorer Christopher Columbus, who had a dream that he could sail a ship all the way across the Atlantic Ocean. People said he was crazy, but Columbus did not know the meaning of the word "discouragement." (He also did not know the meaning of "nostril" or "weasel," because he spoke Italian.)

And so Columbus boldly set out and discovered the New World, and then he went back to Europe, where he died in obscurity at age 55, which is *only five years older than I am right now! OH GOD! MY LIFE IS OVER!!!*

No, scratch that. I really *am* going to be positive in this book, instead of dwelling on the negative aspects of turning 50, such as that you get wrinkled and forgetful and achy, and you gain weight merely by watching food commercials, and the warranties are expiring on all your remaining teeth and internal organs, and your idea of a big night is to stay up late enough to see the *previews* for Letterman, whose actual show you have not watched since the Reagan administration.

I am not going to dwell on those things, nor am I going to mention the fact that when you get to this age, you discover random hairs sprouting from unexpected sectors of your body, so that, in addition to all the other little maintenance tasks you've always performed each day, you find yourself asking questions like: *Did I remember to pluck my ears?*

And I am not going to even mention the word "prostate."

Instead, I'm going to talk about the *good* things that happen to you when you turn 50, such as . . .

Okay, give me a minute here . . .

All right, here's one: You can't read anything. At least I can't. Actually, this started happening to me when I was 48; I started noticing that when I tried to read restaurant menus, they looked like this:

Entrees

Broasted free-range fennel shootlets with modules of prawn — $19

Pecan-encrusted apricot-glazed garlic-enhanced shank of frog — $27

Liver "en Fester" dans une bunche de crème de corne — $21

Introduction

At first I thought that this had nothing to do with me—that, for some reason, possibly to save ink, the restaurants had started printing their menus in letters the height of bacteria; all I could see was little blurs. But for some reason, everybody else seemed to be able to read the menus. Not wishing to draw attention to myself, I started ordering my food by simply pointing to a likely looking blur.

ME (pointing to a blur): I'll have this.
WAITER: You'll have "We Do Not Accept Personal Checks"?
ME: Make that medium rare.

Pretty soon I started noticing that everything I tried to read—newspapers, books, nasal-spray instructions, the United States Constitution—had been changed to the bacteria-letter format. I also discovered that, contrary to common sense, I *could* read these letters if I got *farther away* from them.[1] So for a while I dealt with the situation by ordering off the menus of people sitting at other tables.

"I'd like to order some dessert," I'd tell the waiter. "Please bring a menu to the people at that table over there and ask them to hold it up so I can see it."

Eventually I had to break down and buy those reading glasses that are cut low so you can peer over the top. The first time you put on a pair of those is a major milestone in your life. Because there is no question about it: This is the start of your Senior Citizenship. The transformation is comparable to

---

1. I still don't really understand why this is. My theory is that when the light leaves the printed page, it's young and thin; but after a few feet, it gets older and fatter, and you can see it more easily.

the one Clark Kent goes through: He takes *off* his glasses and becomes Superman; you put *on* your reading glasses and become . . . Old Person.

You find that with your reading glasses on you behave differently. You become crotchety and easily irritated by little things, such as when the supermarket runs out of your preferred brand of low-fat, low-sodium, vitamin-fortified, calcium-enriched, high-fiber, non-meat "breakfast links" made from tofu and compressed cardboard. You become angry at the radio because it keeps playing songs you hate, which is a LOT of songs, because you basically hate every song written since the Beatles broke up, and you're sick of the Beatles, too, because you've heard every one of their songs 900 million times on "oldies" radio, which is all you've listened to for over twenty years. You feel that everybody except you drives too fast. You think of people under the age of 30 as "whippersnappers," and you get the urge to peer over your glasses at them and tell them how tough things were during the Great Depression, even though you personally were born in 1947. Sometimes you are tempted to say, "Con-SARN it!"

So, to avoid transforming into Old Person, you tend to wear your reading glasses as little as possible. You lose them. You go out without them. The result is, much of the time, you can't read anything printed in letters smaller than Marlon Brando.

But what I've discovered—this is the positive aspect of aging that I've been driving at—is that very often not being able to read is a *good thing*. For example, without my reading glasses, the only part of the newspaper I can read is the headlines, so my front page looks like this:

FIGHTING ERUPTS YET AGAIN IN MIDDLE EAST

Historic Peace Accord No. 2,965,978 Goes Down the Crapper

This doesn't say anything. This is just a bunch of words I wrote here to make it look like there's a story under the headline. If you have gone to the trouble of blowing this up so that you can read it, let me just say Congratulations, you have even more spare time than I do, which is saying a LOT.

But seriously, I really have absolutely nothing to tell you here, unless you want me to solve some mysteries that have totally baffled the human race, such as what is the true meaning of life, and whether there is intelligent life elsewhere in the universe and which, really, is the best long-distance carrier for you. Would you like me to tell you those things? You would? OK! I will, then! But first I want to tell you exactly who was responsible for the Kennedy assassination. Ready? Here goes. The Kennedy assassination was committed by

This doesn't say anything. This is just a bunch of words I wrote here to make it look like there's a story under the headline. If you have gone to the trouble of blowing this up so that you can read it, let me just say Congratulations, you have even more spare time than I do, which is saying a LOT.

But seriously, I really have absolutely nothing to tell you here, unless you want me to solve some mysteries that have totally baffled the human race, such as what is the true meaning of life, and whether there is intelligent life elsewhere in the universe and which, really, is the best long-distance carrier for you. Would you like me to tell you those things? You would? OK! I will, then! But first I want to tell you exactly who was responsible for the Kennedy assassination. Ready? Here goes. The Kennedy assassination was committed by

This doesn't say anything. This is just a bunch of words I wrote here to make it look like there's a story under the headline. If you have gone to the trouble of blowing this up so that you can read it, let me just say Congratulations, you have even more spare time than I do, which is saying a LOT.

But seriously, I really have absolutely nothing to tell you here, unless you want me to solve some mysteries that have totally baffled the human race, such as what is the true meaning of life, and whether there is intelligent life elsewhere in the universe and which, really, is the best long-distance carrier for you. Would you like me to tell you those things? You would? OK! I will, then! But first I want to tell you exactly who was responsible for the Kennedy assassination. Ready? Here goes. The Kennedy assassination was committed by

SOCIAL SECURITY SYSTEM COLLAPSING

You, Personally, Will Never Get a Cent HAHAHAHAHAHA

This doesn't say anything. This is just a bunch of words I wrote here to make it look like there's a story under the headline. If you have gone to the trouble of blowing this up so that you can read it, let me just say Congratulations, you have even more spare time than I do, which is saying a LOT.

But seriously, I really have absolutely nothing to tell you here, unless you want me to solve some mysteries that have totally baffled the human race, such as what is the true meaning of life, and whether there is intelligent life elsewhere in the universe and which, really, is the best long-distance carrier for you. Would you like me to tell you those things? You would? OK! I will, then! But first I want to tell you exactly who was responsible for the Kennedy assassination. Ready? Here goes. The Kennedy assassination was committed by

This doesn't say anything. This is just a bunch of words I wrote here to make it look like there's a story under the headline. If you have gone to the trouble of blowing this up so that you can read it, let me just say Congratulations, you have even more spare time than I do, which is saying a LOT.

But seriously, I really have absolutely nothing to tell you here, unless you want me to solve some mysteries that have totally baffled the human race, such as what is the true meaning of life, and whether there is intelligent life elsewhere in the universe and which, really, is the best long-distance carrier for you. Would you like me to tell you those things? You would? OK! I will, then! But first I want to tell you exactly who was responsible for the Kennedy assassination. Ready? Here goes. The Kennedy assassination was committed by

This doesn't say anything. This is just a bunch of words I wrote here to make it look like there's a story under the headline. If you have gone to the trouble of blowing this up so that you can read it, let me just say Congratulations, you have even more spare time than I do, which is saying a LOT.

STUDY: EGGPLANT CAUSES CANCER

Same Study Also Shows That Lack of Eggplant Causes Cancer

But seriously, I really have absolutely nothing to tell you here, unless you want me to solve some mysteries that have totally baffled the human race, such as what is the true meaning of life, and whether there is intelligent life elsewhere in the universe and which, really, is the best long-distance carrier for you. Would you like me to tell you those things? You would? OK! I will, then! But first I want to tell you exactly who was responsible for the Kennedy assassination. Ready? Here goes. The Kennedy assassination was committed by

This doesn't say anything. This is just a bunch of words I wrote here to make it look like there's a story under the headline. If you have gone to the trouble of blowing this up so that you can read it, let me just say Congratulations, you have even more spare time than I do, which is saying a LOT.

But seriously, I really have absolutely nothing to tell you here, unless you want me to solve some mysteries that have totally baffled the human race, such as what is the true meaning of life, and whether there is intelligent life elsewhere in the universe and which, really, is the best long-distance carrier for you. Would you like me to tell you those things? You would? OK! I will, then! But first I want to tell you exactly who was responsible for the Kennedy assassination. Ready? Here goes. The Kennedy assassination was committed by

This doesn't say anything. This is just a bunch of words I wrote here to make it look like there's a story under the headline. If you have gone to the trouble of blowing this up so that you can read it, let me just say Congratulations, you have even more spare time than I do, which is saying a LOT.

GIANT ASTEROID WILL SMASH EARTH TODAY; HUMAN RACE DOOMED

Professional Baseball Players Strike for Higher Salaries

This doesn't say anything. This is just a bunch of words I wrote here to make it look like there's a story under the headline. If you have gone to the trouble of blowing this up so that you can read it, let me just say Congratulations, you have even more spare time than I do, which is saying a LOT.

But seriously, I really have absolutely nothing to tell you here, unless you want me to solve some mysteries that have totally baffled the human race, such as what is the true meaning of life, and whether there is intelligent life elsewhere in the universe and which, really, is the best long-distance carrier for you. Would you like me to tell you those things? You would? OK! I will, then! But first I want to tell you exactly who was responsible for the Kennedy assassination. Ready? Here goes. The Kennedy assassination was committed by

This doesn't say anything. This is just a bunch of words I wrote here to make it look like there's a story under the headline. If you have gone to the trouble of blowing this up so that you can read it, let me just say Congratulations, you have even more spare time than I do, which is saying a LOT.

But seriously, I really have absolutely nothing to tell you here, unless you want me to solve some mysteries that have totally baffled the human race, such as what is the true meaning of life, and whether there is intelligent life elsewhere in the universe and which, really, is the

See what I mean? I don't *want* to read those stories. I'm *glad* they're written in bacteria letters. This is also how I feel about the long, scary Consumer Advisories that appear on virtually every product I buy, advising me how potentially deadly it is, like this:

> **WARNING: Use of this product may cause nausea, insomnia, euphoria, déjà vu, menopause, tax audits, demonic possession, lung flukes, eyeball worms, decapitation, and mudslides. We would not even dare to sell this product if we did not have a huge, carnivorous legal department that could squash you in court like a baby mouse under a sledgehammer. We frankly cannot believe that you were so stupid as to purchase this product. Your only hope is to set this product down very gently, back slowly away from it, then turn and sprint from your home, never to return.**

Back when I could read without reading glasses, I would glance at this information, and it made me nervous. But now, thanks to old age, it looks like this:

> **WARNING:**

So I can just cheerfully discard the Consumer Advisory and swallow the product. Granted, this is sometimes a poor decision, such as when the product is liquid drain opener. But I feel the trade-off is worth it.

I am also much more comfortable these days with products that come in boxes marked "Ready to Assemble." As you consumers know, "Ready to Assemble" is shorthand for "Contains the Same Number of Parts as a Nuclear Aircraft Carrier."

These products used to intimidate me, because the instructions usually consist of hundreds of steps like this:

STEP ONE. *[illegible microtext]*

STEP TWO. *[illegible microtext]*

STEP THREE. *[illegible microtext]*

STEP FOUR. *[illegible microtext]*

GO BACK TO STEP ONE. *[illegible microtext]*

But these days I just toss the instructions aside and start assembling the product. And you know what? I've found that, using nothing but my common sense and natural mechanical ability, I actually finish the assembly process *faster* than before! Granted, most of the time the products don't work. But they rarely worked even when I *could* read the instructions, so I figure I'm ahead.

And the inability to read is not the only good thing about turning 50. There's also the fact that you've reached the point in life where you accept the fact that you cannot possibly be hip.

Actually, I don't even know whether "hip" is the word for hip anymore. And I don't have to care! That's the point! Even if I knew how to talk hip, or dress hip, or listen to hip music— even if I knew *everything* about what currently, at this particular nanosecond in our culture constitutes hipness—I am still, on account of my age, automatically disqualified. What a relief! I'm over the Hipness Hump!

I can remember when I wasn't. There was a brief period, during my college years, when as far as I can tell, I actually *was* kind of hip, as measured by the standards of The Sixties.[2] Then I went through a long, murky phase—from my 20s through my 40s—when my hipness was steadily draining away, but I would still feel a nagging obligation to participate in trends. The problem was that, as an aging person, I was no longer capable of distinguishing between the trends that were in fact hip and the ones that were just stupid.

For example, do you remember the period—I think it was during the Seventies—when some guys would turn up the collars on their sports jackets? The first time I saw this look—it was on a guy in an elevator in New York City—I thought it was a mistake, and I told the guy, as a friendly gesture, "Your jacket collar is up." He looked at me as though I were a manure-encrusted pig farmer who had just told him that ice was actually frozen water.

"I *know*," he said.

After that, I started seeing a lot of guys with their collars up, and I realized that it was a trend. Many of these guys were younger than I, but some were my age or even older, and I wondered: Should *I* be doing this? When I was young and hip—when it was a question of wearing bell-bottomed jeans, or growing my hair long, or smoking banana skins to see if

---

2. Actually, there *were* no standards in The Sixties; that was the point.

they got you high[3]—I never had a moment's doubt; I just *knew*. But I was ambivalent about the turned-up jacket collar: Was it really hip? Or were these guys just a bunch of twits?

The answer, we now know thanks to tests conducted by the National Institute of Science, is that they were in fact a bunch of twits. So I'm glad I never participated in that trend. But the point is that, because of my Hipness Uncertainty Syndrome, I wasted valuable time worrying about it.

As years passed and I got older, I found myself worrying less and less about trends. For example, when I was in my 40s, young black men started wearing their baseball caps backward. I was never even slightly tempted to imitate them. A lot of guys were, though. It wasn't so bad with the younger ones, but there was a certain age—I would pinpoint this age at 17— beyond which it started to look pretty silly. You'd see middle-class white guys in their 30s apparently thinking that by turning their caps around they had transformed themselves from junior insurance executives into bad ghetto dudes. Boyz N the Burbz.

I'm happy that, as a definitely older person, I'll never again have to go through that. Likewise I never have to wonder if I should try to like rap music, or wear gigantic pants with the waist down around my knees. Nor do I ever feel any need to participate in a current trend with potentially a very high twitness quotient: Cigar Mania, which in the mid-Nineties swept the nation the way a fart sweeps a crowded living room. All of a sudden, everywhere you go, all these people in the prime of

---

3. No.

their Hipness Uncertainty Syndrome years are fondling cigars, puffing earnestly away on cigars, and—worst of all—droning away endlessly about cigars, as though cigars are an intellectual topic comparable to classical literature, as opposed to transient wads of spit-drenched tobacco.

Don't misunderstand me: I know that some people, a small minority, truly *like* cigars—they smoked them before they were popular, and they'll smoke them after they stop being popular. But you just know that, at some point, a whole lot of these puffers and fondlers and droners are going to wake up one morning, smell the cigar stench on their hair and skin and taste the cigar slime clinging to their teeth, and they're going to say: "What the hell am I *doing?*"

Most of us older people managed to completely avoid participating in the cigar trend, and we feel good about it. We also feel good about the fact that when we hear about global warming, or toxic waste, or global cooling, or the destruction of the rain forests, or one of the many other serious problems threatening to wipe out the entire human race by the year 2050 unless we do something drastic, we can frown politely as though we're concerned, when in fact we're thinking: "No problem! I'll be dead!"

Yes, there are some real benefits to turning 50. And that's going to be the theme of this book: It's going to be a *celebration* of the aging process. I'm not talking about just my aging process, but that of the whole massive Baby Boom Generation— the millions and millions of us who were born in the postwar era and went on to set a standard for whiny self-absorption that probably will never be equaled.

But dammit, we have a lot to be self-absorbed *about*. Oh, sure, we had a pretty impressive act to follow. Our parents' generation overcame the Great Depression, won World War II, and went on to build the greatest and most powerful nation this planet has ever seen. But look at the many accomplishments that we Baby Boomers can point to: *Saturday Night Live!* The New Age movement! Call waiting!

And those are only a few examples. There will be many more in this book, which will chart the historic, highlight-studded course of the Boomers—from the days when they wore diapers to the heady days, decades later, when, as the dominant generation of the planet's dominant nation, they are starting to wear diapers again.

Come, fellow Boomer. Take my hand, and let us travel together on a voyage of exploration into our very favorite topic, which is us. Let us examine in detail the questions of who we are, and where we came from, and where we are going. I promise you that it will be a fascinating journey. Simply read on, and we shall begin.

But first, let go of my hand, because it's really hard to type this way.

QUIZ: HOW OLD ARE YOU?

1. Describe your family's first TV set.
 a. It was a huge wooden cabinet with two big knobs and a teensy screen featuring a black-and-white picture that I rarely saw because my dad was always standing in front of it adjusting the rabbit-ear antenna and saying bad words.
 b. It was a Sony.

2. *Who was featured on your first lunchbox?*
   a. Davy Crockett.
   b. Vanilla Ice.

3. *Do you remember Howdy Doody?*
   a. Of course.
   b. You are making that name up.

4. *Who was the first living U.S. president whom you were aware of?*
   a. Harry Truman.
   b. Vanilla Ice.

5. *Did you ever, personally, own a 78 r.p.m. record?*
   a. Yes.
   b. A *what?*

6. *Did you, later on, own a whole batch of 45 r.p.m. records that you wrote your name on the labels of and kept in a carrying case that had a handle? And you put little plastic inserts in the holes?*
   a. Yes.
   b. Why did you need little plastic inserts for the holes?

7. *Have you ever thought that* Beavis and Butt-Head *is funny?*
   a. No.
   b. Yes, I am always amused when they burp and go *heheheheheh.*

8. *Do you remember when there were no area codes? And there was only one gigantic Soviet Union–style telephone company? And all*

the phones were black and they belonged to the phone company and if you wanted to get a new one you had to wait in your house like a prisoner for days at a time until the phone company, taking its sweet time, decided to install one, as opposed to now, when they sell telephones at drugstores, as if they were breath mints? And do you remember a time when you weren't incessantly bombarded with advertising about your long-distance options, because there WEREN'T any long-distance options? And phone numbers had letters at the beginning, reflecting your area of residence, such as (in my personal case) ARmonk 3, 3119, which made the numbers easier to remember? Do you think that one reason why children today can't remember their multiplication tables is that they have to remember seven-digit phone numbers for their homes, plus their parents' cell phones and beepers; not to mention their home alarm codes and various random PIN numbers; on top of which somebody—possibly hostile space aliens—keeps adding NEW area codes every other week, so that some day we're going to have a separate area code for every single household in America *and our brains will be so full of numbers that one day our skulls will start spontaneously exploding and people will try to call for help but they won't be able to remember the seventeen-digit number that will no doubt soon replace 911?*

a. Yes.

b. You're saying there *didn't used to be area codes?*

9. *Do you remember when pop singing stars with major hit records would go on TV shows—most notably Dick Clark's* American Bandstand*—and the teenagers (the girls wearing sweaters; the*

boys wearing skinny ties) would dance the Stroll while the stars would lip-synch their records hilariously badly, as though they were hearing the songs for the first time?
a. Yes.
b. Dick Clark? The sweepstakes guy?

10. *Did you ever do the Slop?*
    a. Of course.
    b. The *what?*

11. *Did you ever do the Humpty Dance?*
    a. The *what?*
    b. Of course.

12. *Do you remember when "boss" was a popular slang term denoting approval, as in "Duane got a boss GTO"?*
    a. Yes.
    b. That is *pathetic.*

13. *Who was Winky Dink?*
    a. A cartoon character that you got out of trouble by drawing lines on a plastic thing you put on your TV screen.
    b. I'll agree with "a" on this one.
    c. Hey! That's cheating!

14. *Where were you the first time you heard the Beatles?*
    a. In a station wagon.
    b. In a fallopian tube.

15. Did you ever experiment with drugs?
a. No.
b. No.

HOW TO SCORE

Count the number of "a" answers, then refer to the following handy chart:

YOUR SCORE	HOW OLD YOU ARE
You can ignore this.	This is just another joke based on using unreadably small type.
There will probably be a lot of them in this book.	Let's hope I eventually get bored with this idea.

If you can't read the handy chart, you're old. But you knew that.

2
The Early History
of the Boomers

Hey, the World Wasn't Exactly Perfect When We Got Here.

The history of the Baby Boom generation is really the history of the entire species; for if we are to truly understand the Boomers, we must view them not as an isolated phenomenon, but as the result of all that went before them. And thus we must begin our story by traveling back in time millions of years, to the moment when the very first human being appeared on Earth. After that a whole bunch of stuff happened, which leads us to . . .

1947

This is the historic year when the first Boomers were born. The reason there were so many of us was that our parents' generation, having endured the misery of the Depression and the horror of the war years, evidently spent much of 1946 in the sack. At the time, they thought they were merely starting families, as humans had done for eons; they had no way of knowing that they were creating a unique, historic generation. If they *had* known, probably a lot more of them would have opted to join celibate religious orders. But by the time they realized what they had let loose on the world, it was too late.

I don't remember many specifics about 1947, because I spent that year burping up milk. But judging from my family's old photos, I would say that 1947 was an era when the men wore suits, the women held the babies, everybody smoked cigarettes, and the entire world was yellowish and curling up at the edges.

Most of the cars were black. All the kitchen appliances and elected officials were white.

A hit song was "Peg O' My Heart," by the Harmonicats.[1]

The president was Harry Truman, an older man who wore formal hats and wire-rimmed glasses. In fact the whole world was run by older men who wore formal hats and wire-rimmed glasses. People saw them mainly in newsreels, waving to the cameras before going into historic conferences, where they held secret high-level negotiations and talked fashion ("Your formal hat looks great!" "Thanks! Yours, too!" "We're going to invade Hungary!" "Okay!").

My parents, David and Marion, turned 30 in 1947. They look astonishingly young to me in the photos, although my dad was already bald. (He was born bald, and he went bald

---

1. Do you think they put that on their income-tax returns? (Occupation: Harmonicat.)

again at a very young age. There are very few photographs of my dad with hair.) My dad was a Presbyterian minister, and my mom was—this word had no negative connotations in 1947—a housewife. The year I was born they started building the house I grew up in, in Armonk, New York, a small town about thirty miles from New York City, where my dad worked at a social service agency called the New York City Mission Society.

My parents didn't have much money, so my dad did a lot of the work on our house himself; he kept working on it through much of my childhood, so there were always unfinished rooms, and we Barry kids (there eventually were four of us) played on piles of lumber. My dad was not a natural craftsman, but he'd try anything—carpentry, electrical wiring, plumbing, roofing. From watching him, I learned a lesson that still applies to my life today: No matter how difficult a task may seem, if you're not afraid to try it—and if you really put your mind to it—*you can do it.* And when you're done, it will leak.

But getting back to 1947: While I was being born and my parents, like millions of other young couples, were carving out a new life in the suburbs, two developments of historic global significance were taking place:

1. The postwar power struggle between the United States and the Soviet Union was escalating into the Cold War, bringing with it the constant, looming threat that human civilization itself could be destroyed in an unthinkable nuclear holocaust.
2. History's first aerosol food product—Reddi-Wip—was being invented.

A third development that was to have a huge impact on the Baby Boom generation—television—was still in its infancy (except for Mike Wallace, who was already 73 years old). Few American households had TV sets, and there wasn't much in the way of programming—mainly variety shows, a few situation comedies,[2] and a commercial for an early, kerosene-powered Salad Shooter. The dominant electronic medium back then was radio, which was still delighting Americans with shows such as "Fibber McGee & Molly," which as I understand it concerned the hilarious antics of a guy with a lot of stuff in a closet.[3]

So basically, despite some unnerving international developments, the mood of 1947, for my parents' generation, was "the war is finally over, so let's settle down and enjoy peace and prosperity." Many of them got their prosperity, but thanks to my generation, they did not get much peace.

What happened? Why did we Boomers turn out the way we did—so loud; so self-absorbed; so cocky; so trend-driven; so eager to disrespect, disobey, and shock; so determinedly *different* from the generations before us? Could our arrival be somehow related to the fact that 1947 was also the first year that large numbers of people claimed to have seen UFOs? Did alien beings, realizing that humans were on the verge of great technological advancement, send spacecraft here to bombard the huge batch of postwar babies with some kind of ray that caused a psychological mutation, so that years later, just as the human race was developing the technology to travel into

---

2. Starring Tony Danza.
3. This is also the plot of *War and Peace.*

space, the Baby Boomers took over, and humanity's focus shifted from exploring the universe to developing a workable home espresso machine?

We may never know the answer. I'm not sure I understand the *question*. Besides which, if we're ever going to get back to the present day and the whole issue of turning 50, we need to move past 1947 and look at what happened in . . .

1948

For one thing, the Cold War got a lot hotter with the Soviet blockade of Berlin, which the Allies countered with the Berlin Airlift.[4] These events reinforced a fundamental theme of Boomer childhood—that the Communists were our mortal enemies, a relentless, evil, sneaky, beady-eyed threat, always trying to infiltrate us and destroy us and our values[5] and our cherished way of life. Way before we had any clear idea what "Communism" was, my friends and I played a game called "G-Man," in which we'd run around making shooting noises and calling each other "Commie!" As it turns out, major U.S. political figures were doing pretty much the same thing at that time, although of course they didn't make shooting noises, because their teeth would have fallen out.

---

4. The Berlin Airlift involved attaching the city of Berlin via stout cables to Air Force bombers, picking it up, and flying it to safety—a feat that would have been impossible without fantastic quantities of beer.
5. One of our cherished values in those days was that if you went swimming within an hour after eating, you'd get a cramp and die. The Communists required *two* hours.

In other foreign news from 1948, Queen Elizabeth II of England gave birth to an heir and charter member of the Space Cadet Academy, Charles Philip Arthur George William Ted Bob, who would be rigorously educated and trained in his duties as prince, so that one day, when the time was right, he could become a much older prince.

The year 1948 also saw some important advances in technology. In those days, office workers had to make duplicate documents using messy, inconvenient carbon paper. But on October 22, a small company in Rochester, New York, gave the first public demonstration of what would become known around the world as "the Xerox® brand copier." This was followed immediately by the first demonstration of what would become known around the world as "calling the guy to fix the damned Xerox® brand copier," after which everybody went back to using messy, inconvenient carbon paper for several more decades.

Another important technological breakthrough came from the musical-recording industry. At the time, everybody used 78 r.p.m. records, which spun around really fast, which meant that these records could hold only short songs, which meant that these records were not well suited for use as make-out music.

THE SCENE: A man and woman are alone in an apartment at the end of a romantic evening of dining and dancing. The man lowers the lights, puts a 78 r.p.m. record of "Smoke Gets in Your Eyes" on the phonograph, then goes over to the woman, who is sitting on the sofa. He puts his arm around her and turns his face toward hers. Her lips are parted in anticipation. The record ends.

MAN: Excuse me a second.

(He gets up, goes back over to the phonograph, takes off "Smoke Gets in Your Eyes," puts on "On a Slow Boat to China," returns to the sofa, and puts his arm around the woman. The record ends.)

MAN: Excuse me a second.

(He gets up, goes back over to the phonograph, takes off "On a Slow Boat to China," puts on "Near You," returns to the sofa, and puts his arm around the woman. The record ends.)

MAN: Excuse me a second.

WOMAN: Zzzzzzzzz

It's a tribute to the horniness of our parents' generation that they *ever* managed to have sex during the 78 r.p.m. era. But things changed dramatically in 1948 with the introduction of two new formats: (1) 45 r.p.m.; and (2) for the real make-out artists, the $33\frac{1}{3}$ r.p.m., or "Long Playing," format. This meant that the Baby Boomers grew up with *three* record formats, one of which, the 45 r.p.m., had—and this *still* baffles top scientists—a much bigger hole than the other two.

The result of all these formats was that the record players we used had to be real contraptions. For one thing, they had three speeds,[6] with a little lever that you used to change them. Also they had two needles; you flipped the needle thing over, depending on which kind of record you were playing. And when you played a 45 r.p.m. record, you either had to put a

---

6. Actually, as I recall, some of them had *four* speeds, including one called "16," although I never encountered a "16" record. Maybe this had something to do with the Communists.

plastic insert in the hole or attach a special spindle to the record player, sometimes using a hammer.

So when measured against today's high-tech CD stereo systems, the record players of those days were closer in design, and sound quality, to washing machines. Granted, some record players were advertised as being "high fidelity," but this meant only that you could usually identify the gender of the singer in less than three verses.

On the plus side, the old record players enabled you, the listener, to play a more active role in the music. You could, for example, play a 33⅓ record at 45, or even 78, so that Frank Sinatra sounded like a singing hamster. You could put a 45 r.p.m. record on without a plastic insert, so it was off center on the turntable, which created a very comical effect until your mom came into the living room and threatened to smack you with a broom. Then it was time to go outside and play "G-Man."

Perhaps the biggest technological event of 1948 was the first public demonstration of the transistor, an amazing device that . . . umm . . . Okay, to be honest, I have no idea what specific amazing thing the transistor does. I do know that it eventually replaced "tubes," which were glowing glass objects found inside the record players, radios, and TVs of my youth. In those days, if there was a problem, you'd unplug your tubes and take them down to the hardware store, where there was a big box called a tube tester, and you'd test your tubes, and if necessary buy new ones—they sold tubes right at the hardware store—and you'd put them in your radio or record player or TV, and sometimes it would actually work again. Now, of course, thanks to the miracle of the transistor, if anything goes wrong with an electronic device it can be fixed only by the factory, which is located in Taiwan, so you just throw it away and buy a new one.

And speaking of modern conveniences: 1948 was the year the first McDonald's restaurant opened, thus beginning the era of "fast food." The concept was simple: Instead of forcing customers to waste valuable time waiting while their orders were prepared from fresh ingredients, the restaurant decided ahead of time what the customers wanted (they wanted meat fried in grease, with a side order of potatoes fried in grease) and prepared the food well in advance (some of the original McDonald's hamburgers are still in circulation today). Thus the busy customers, hard-pressed to keep up with the rapid pace of modern life, could simply walk in, grab their food, eat it, walk out, and fall over dead with arteries clogged to the density of Genoa salami.

On the cultural front 1948 saw the debut of what some of us consider to be one of the greatest shows ever to appear on television: *Ted Mack's Original Amateur Hour.* This was a show that gave real meaning to the word "amateur," defined as "a person who is not being paid to perform, and you can see why."

My father *loved* the *Original Amateur Hour.* He and I would be watching it on our RCA Victor combination TV and record player with the gigantic wooden cabinet and the tiny screen, and one of the contestants on the show would be, say, a young woman from Brooklyn who played the xylophone, and she'd be performing a song such as "Flight of the Bumblebee" (*Amateur Hour* contestants were *always* playing "Flight of the

Bumblebee"; speed was considered the most important component of a musical performance). The woman would be flailing away at the xylophone, and my dad would yell, "Behind your back! Play it behind your back!" And the woman—it was as if she could hear my dad right through the TV screen—would suddenly turn sideways, whip one arm around behind her, and *play the xylophone behind her back,* and my dad and I would cheer like maniacs.

You don't see entertainment like that anymore.

My family actually had a close personal brush with the *Original Amateur Hour.* This happened in the mid-1950s, when my cousin John Gladieux, who lived in Milwaukee, competed on the show playing the flute. The *Amateur Hour* was broadcast from New York, so the night before John performed, he stayed at our house in Armonk. He was due to arrive right around dinnertime; my mother was cooking, in a double boiler, one of her special dishes, creamed chipped beef,[7] and we kids were very excited about hosting our TV-star cousin.

Finally there came a knock on the door, and we all ran to greet John. Just as he walked in, there was a very loud noise from the kitchen. This turned out to be the double boiler exploding. You have no idea how many square feet of surface coverage you can get from a pot of creamed chipped beef until you see it with your own eyes. There was creamed chipped beef dripping down all four walls and from every part of the ceiling.

---

7. I have heard a lot of people, especially people who have been exposed to military cooking, make disparaging remarks about creamed chipped beef, but my mom's was excellent. Perhaps this was because she never served in the military.

Creamed chipped beef had been hurled at high velocity deep into every corner and crevice and appliance and light fixture. It was one of the most memorable sights of my entire childhood, and to add to the general excitement, the next day my cousin John—perhaps still feeling the adrenaline rush of the previous night—went on to *win* the *Amateur Hour* competition. It was a huge thrill for the Barry household, almost compensating for the way the kitchen smelled.

In other cultural events, 1948 saw the debut of *Pogo,* which is by actual scientific measurement one of the greatest comic strips of all time. Also appearing that year was the first animated TV commercial, featuring the first major TV jingle, for Ajax ("Use Ajax! The foaming cleanser!"). This would be followed by thousands more jingles and commercial slogans, which gradually would fill the Baby Boomers' minds with what I call "brain sludge," the result being that as we enter our 50s, most of us cannot name the secretary of defense,[8] but we can still sing the Mister Clean song.

But as impressive as the events and accomplishments of 1948 were, they would pale beside a discovery that would be made in . . .

1949

I'm sure that I don't need to remind you what happened in 1949. I'm sure you know that 1949 will forever be remembered

---

8. Tony Danza.

by grateful future generations as "the year that Silly Putty was first marketed."

It's difficult to imagine what human life was like before this product became available. We can only speculate how history would have differed if our ancestors had possessed it.

THE SCENE: Philadelphia, Pennsylvania, 1787
JAMES MADISON: And so we must include a Bill of Rights to guarantee that . . .
BENJAMIN FRANKLIN: Hey, look! When you press this stuff down on the Constitution, then pull it off, you can see the letters on it backward!
ALEXANDER HAMILTON: Hey, look what happens when you stretch it! Ha ha!
MADISON: But we really need to include a . . .
GEORGE WASHINGTON: You're out of order, Madison! *(To the others:)* Let's adjourn and see if this stuff bounces!

Speaking of technological breakthroughs, 1949 saw the first direct-dialed long-distance telephone call, between New York and San Francisco. Of course, back in that primitive era the parties had to speak to each other manually; today one or both ends of the conversation would be carried on by a machine.

Another major advance making its first appearance in 1948 was the Oreo cookie. I, personally, ate 461 million Oreos in my childhood, often using the Disassembly Technique, wherein you start by taking the two wafers apart and licking off the cream. I also drank a fair amount of Hershey's syrup directly out of the can. Today I nibble reduced-calorie celery and *still* gain weight.

On the personal-grooming front, 1949 saw the introduction of Brylcreem, which many men (not my dad; he didn't need it) used on their hair when I was growing up. Brylcreem ("A little dab'll do ya") controlled hair the way the Soviet Union controlled East Germany. As I recall, it competed with a product called Wildroot Cream Oil ("Get Wildroot Cream Oil, Chaaarr-leeeee; it keeps your hair in trim!"). Both products gave the user a slick, totally immobile, bullet-deflecting hairstyle with an oily sheen; the average male looked as though if you set his hairstyle on fire, it would burn for days.

Hair discipline was important, back then. Nobody had really long hair. The most radical hair statement for males was the D.A., or "Duck's Ass" hairstyle, featuring sideburns and hair swept back on the sides; this was worn by your juvenile delinquent "hot-rodder" type of hoodlum individual whose morals had been corrupted by reading comic books.

Most males got their hair cut every two weeks. When I was young, my mom took me down to the barbershop on the main street in Armonk, which was run by three Italian men who played Italian-opera records all day. There was a big round wooden table where, while you waited your turn, you could read *Police Gazette,* unless you were with your mom, in which case you read *Field & Stream.*

Haircuts cost a quarter, and over the mirror were pictures of the styles available, which included the "Continental," the "Hollywood," and the "Crew Cut." I secretly wanted the "Hollywood," but my mom always told the barber to give me the

"Crew Cut," which basically meant cutting all the hairs on the head to a height of about three-eighths of an inch. It's similar to the style worn by tennis balls.

When I got a little older, my dad—this was one of the more tragic developments of my childhood—brought home a pair of electric clippers that he got at a drugstore in Grand Central Station. For the next few years, my dad—who was the finest human being I have ever known, but who had the hairstyling skills and fashion flair of a lathe operator—cut my hair, as well as the hair of my brothers Phil and Sam. This meant that I spent my critical junior high school years underneath what looked like the pelt of some very sick rodent.

But getting back to the events of 1949: This was also the year that the Russians, by cheating, got the atomic bomb, which was very bad because we knew that if they had the opportunity they would fly over here and drop it on our cherished way of life. And thus one of the defining experiences of Boomer childhood would come to be the nuclear-attack drill at school, wherein the teachers had us kids practice protecting ourselves by crouching under our desks, which were apparently made out of some kind of atomic-bomb-proof wood.

The constant somewhere-in-the-back-of-your-mind fear of nuclear attack was a very big part of our childhoods, especially in the 1950s. I'm not saying we perceived it as the same magnitude of threat as, for example, acne, but it was always there, the idea that *any minute now we could all be blown away.* For a while, people—including people we knew—were building bomb shelters in their backyards. (My dad never built a bomb shelter, which is just as well, because it would have leaked.)

One time, my best childhood friend, Neil Thompson, and I made "survival kits," which were toolboxes containing flashlights, water, candy bars, and other items that, according to some article we had read, we'd want to have handy when the nuclear attack came. We waited for several days, but the attack (you never could trust the Russians) failed to come, so we went ahead and ate the candy bars.

In the arts, 1949 brought good news and bad news:

The good news included the first Mister Magoo cartoon, and the fact that B. B. King started making records. So did Fats Domino, which meant that even though the world wasn't yet ready for rock and roll, steps were being taken in the right direction. And 1949 saw the beginning of one of my favorite early-childhood TV shows, *Captain Video,* about a courageous adventurer of the future, flying around the universe in a spacecraft made entirely out of cheap props.

Also appearing on TV for the first time that year were two other shows I never missed: *Hopalong Cassidy,* who was a good guy even though he wore a black outfit; and *The Lone Ranger,* who we kids thought for years was the *Long* Ranger, and who was a good guy even though he wore a mask. We kids thought the mask was cool, although we never really understood its purpose. I mean, it didn't really *disguise* the Lone Ranger, any more than Superman disguised himself when he put glasses on and pretended to be Clark Kent. Looking back on it, I suspect that the ordinary townsfolk—the people whom the Lone Ranger was always rescuing from bad guys—probably thought, deep down inside, that he was pretty weird, with his mask and everything. They were probably somewhat relieved when he galloped away at the end with his faithful Indian companion, Tonto.

But as I say, we thought the Lone Ranger was very cool, and we spent countless hours emulating him and Hopalong Cassidy and, later on, Roy Rogers. The way we emulated them was by shooting cap guns, which were hugely popular then, even though the rolls of cap paper were always jamming and misfiring. My friends and I would stand around shooting at each other from a range of two feet or less, our guns occasionally going "bang," but usually just emitting a pathetic *"click"* or *"phhtt."* We argued constantly about who was dead, and about who was the good guy and who was the bad guy. Nobody was ever the faithful Indian companion.

Culturally, the bad news from 1949 was that Gene Autrey recorded "Rudolph the Red-Nosed Reindeer." I'm not saying this is a bad song; I'm just saying that there should be a legal limitation on it, so that if you're shopping in a mall during the holiday season, and "Rudolph the Red-Nosed Reindeer" comes on the public address system more than three times in a one-hour period, the mall manager should be assessed some kind of penalty, such as death.

But overall, 1949 was a fine year, a year of transition from the World War II decade to the decade of the Fifties, in which the Boomers would begin to define themselves as a major cultural force, and also acquire lunchboxes.

DISCUSSION QUESTIONS—THE FORTIES

Can you imagine your parents having sex? I can. (Imagine your parents, I mean.)

Did you ever spray Reddi-Wip directly into your mouth? How about your dog's mouth? Explain.

3
The Fifties

Domestic Prosperity. International Tension. Buffalo Bob.

lthough the Cold War was raging abroad, at home the Fifties were pretty much a brain-dead decade, dominated by shallow consumerism and silly fads. So it was a *great* time to be a kid. Plus, how can you criticize an era that gave us both the Salk vaccine *and* Little Richard?

So let's hop into our 1957 Plymouth with the tailfins the size of Appalachian foothills, and let's motor up to the Drive-Thru Window of Time to order the Big Greasy Corn Dog of Decades, starting with . . .

1950

If you were to name the two most important personalities of 1950, in terms of their long-term impact on the Boomers, those two names would have to be Richard Nixon and Howdy Doody, although not necessarily in that order.

Howdy Doody was of course the star of *The Howdy Doody Show*, which in 1950 became the nation's number one children's program. Also starring on the show, which was set in—yes—Doodyville, were Buffalo Bob[1] and Clarabell the Clown, who had a wide repertoire of wacky antics, such as squirting people with seltzer. Actually, come to think of it, seltzer-squirting was pretty much Clarabell's entire wacky-antic repertoire, but we young viewers never tired of this plot development.

By this point Americans were buying TV sets like crazy, and most of us Boomers were watching *The Howdy Doody Show* religiously. When Buffalo Bob started the show with his traditional question—"Say, kids, what time is it?"—we shouted at the screen: "IT'S HOWDY DOODY TIME!" We sang the Howdy Doody Song,[2] and we nagged our parents incessantly to buy the many items of Howdy Doody merchandise advertised on it. They could have advertised the official Howdy Doody edition of all sixteen volumes of *Remembrance of Things Past* by Marcel Proust in the original French, and we would have *begged* our parents for it ("Mom, can I please have all sixteen volumes of *Remembrance of Things Past* by Marcel Proust in the original French c'mon please please *PLEASE*").

We also wanted more than anything in the world to be in

---

1. That was his stage name, of course; his real name was Giraffe Bob.
2. When we became older and more mature, we sang the unauthorized version, which went:

> It's Howdy Doody time
> Come get your booty shined
> It only costs a dime
> To get your booty shined!
>
> (Copyright 1953 Neil Diamond)

the Peanut Gallery, which was *The Howdy Doody Show*'s live studio audience. The Peanut Gallery consisted of real kids just like us; I know this because I distinctly remember one show in which a boy in the Peanut Gallery kept raising his hand and shouting "Buffalo Bob! Buffalo Bob!" Finally Buffalo Bob said, "What?" and the boy said, "My brother wet his pants."

Also debuting on TV that year was *What's My Line*, in which a panel of celebrities would try to guess somebody's occupation. This concept seems wonderfully quaint today, when celebrities would not dream of going on TV for any purpose other than to talk about themselves.

Along with the new shows in 1950 came a major technological breakthrough: the laugh track. Thanks to this invention, it was no longer necessary for TV viewers to do the hard mental work involved in figuring out for themselves what parts of a show were supposed to be funny. Now, thanks to the laugh track, they were simply told the answer, which was: *ALL* the parts of the show were supposed to be funny!

For example, before the laugh track, viewers might be uncertain as to the hilarity level of TV-show dialogue such as this:

FIRST CHARACTER: Hi, Bob.
SECOND CHARACTER: Hi, Fred.
FIRST CHARACTER: Nice day.
SECOND CHARACTER: If it doesn't rain.

But all that changed in 1950, when professional humor technicians began alerting us to the funny parts by using a laugh machine to insert chuckles, chortles, guffaws, and major belly laughter where appropriate:

FIRST CHARACTER: IIi, Bob.
LAUGH MACHINE: Chucklechucklechucklechuckle
SECOND CHARACTER: Hi, Fred.
LAUGH MACHINE: Chortlechortlechortlechortle
FIRST CHARACTER: Nice day.
LAUGH MACHINE (barely able to control itself because it senses that a real "zinger" is coming): Guffawguffawguffawguffaw
SECOND CHARACTER: If it doesn't rain.
LAUGH MACHINE (wetting its electronic pants): **HAHAHA HAHAHAHAHAHAHAHAHAHAHAHAHAHAHAHA HAHAHAHAHAHA**

Suddenly, it was possible to produce comedy shows that the viewing audience, without the benefit of the laugh track, would never have recognized as being funny. It was even possible to take a show that had been originally intended as a serious melodrama and, by inserting huge electronic belly laughs into it every thirty seconds, turn it into a "situation comedy." Experts believe this is what happened with *Three's Company,* which was originally intended to be a training film for U.S. Postal Service employees.

Along with the rapid growth of the television industry in 1950 came the rise of a related industry, one that's still going strong today: the industry of people who go around declaring that television is a Bad Thing. Speaking at Boston University's 1950 graduation ceremonies, the university's president, Daniel

Marsh, said: "If the television craze continues with the present level of programs, we are destined to have a nation of morons." These are visionary words indeed, coming from a man who had never seen either Beavis *or* Butt-Head.

Speaking of threats to civilization: 1950 was the year Richard Nixon was elected to Congress. He quickly made a national name for himself by publicly suspecting that everybody except possibly his wife, Pat, was a Communist; he managed to remain a major blip on the nation's political and psychological radar screen for more than forty years. I suspect that a majority of us Boomers, if you polled us, would say the national political figure who *influenced* us the most, at least when we were young, was John Kennedy. But the one we had to *think about* the most—had to try to *comprehend*—was Nixon.

I will admit that I spent a good part of my life despising Richard Nixon. I especially despised him in 1968, when he got himself elected president by claiming that he had a Secret Plan to get us out of Vietnam, and it turned out that this plan was so secret that even Nixon didn't know what it was.

But I also believe that Nixon provided some of the greatest pure entertainment this nation has ever seen. When he was president, if you could disregard the fact that he was (a) the most powerful man in the world and (b) clinically insane, you could really enjoy watching him look into the TV camera, trying SO hard to appear to be a sincere, humanoid life-form— struggling to figure out what to do with his eyes, his mouth, his hands, his voice, looking and sounding like a man whose central nervous system was being remote-controlled from a great distance by alien beings who had gotten all their information on human behavior from watching Boris Karloff movies.

None of us who saw it will ever forget the moment, at the Republican National Convention in 1972, when Nixon and Sammy Davis Jr. hooked up, on stage, for one of history's most entertaining embraces: Mr. Hep Cat meets The Human Fish. And it is unlikely that the Oval Office will ever see a more wondrous occasion than the one in 1970—captured, fortunately, by an official photographer—when President Nixon made Elvis, who had God only knows what coursing through his bloodstream at the time, an honorary federal agent for his work in combating the menace of drugs.

Speaking of menaces, 1950 was the year that Senator Joseph McCarthy of Wisconsin shocked the nation with the announcement that he had a list of Communists who had infiltrated America at the highest levels, and that one of them was: Buffalo Bob.

No, as far as I know Buffalo Bob was never implicated in the Red Scare. But just about everybody else was. Things *were* kind of scary on the international front: The Russians were building more atomic bombs, so President Truman decided that we would go ahead and build the *hydrogen* bomb, which was even more powerful, which meant that eventually the Russians would build it, too, which meant that we youngsters would need even thicker school desks to hide under.

And in 1950 the Korean War began. I remember very little about it—it ended when I was 6—but I do vividly recall one time in 1952, when I was at kindergarten, and a classmate, who had obtained this information from his dad, told me, as we were waiting our turn to swing on the playground swings at Wampus Elementary School, that if we *lost* the Korean War, Chinese Communists would come right into Armonk. I remember standing there, trying to imagine what Chinese Communists would look like, and whether they would let us use the swings, or just hog them all for themselves.

But aside from the imminent threat of invasion, the quality of life continued to improve in 1950. Kellogg's introduced Sugar Pops, which was followed in a couple of years by Kellogg's Sugar Smacks and Kellogg's Sugar Frosted Flakes. They could have come out with a product called Kellogg's Box Full of Sugar with No Cereal in It, and it would have sold like crazy.

That was one of the fun things about being a kid in the 1950s: In stark contrast to today, most people were not obsessed with, or even necessarily aware of, the concept of nutrition. The older generations, remembering the Depression, were thrilled just not to be starving. So we Boomers could eat pretty much anything. After eating a breakfast of sugared cereal—to which we added sugar—we enjoyed a lunch of baloney sandwiches or hot dogs with potato chips and a Twinkie; for dinner our moms made us hearty meals of macaroni and cheese with bread and butter, with chocolate cake and a big glass of milk—we could not drink too much milk in those days—and if anybody had talked about how many "grams" of fat were involved in our diets, we would have thought that person was from Mars.

Needless to say, we also ate tons of candy, including some products that probably were not, technically, food. For example, we ate these little wax bottles filled with some kind of syrup that was so sweet it would probably eat its way through a steel girder in seconds. We ate candy buttons that came on strips of paper, which meant that, to eat the buttons, you also ate a lot of paper. But it was paper with *sugar* on it, so it tasted fine to us. On the beverage front, we had numerous chocolate-sludge drinks such as the relentlessly advertised Bosco ("I love Bosco! That's the drink for me!"). But we also had strange mutant beverages such as "Fizzies," which were these Alka-Seltzer-like tablets that you dropped in water, where they fizzed and turned the water into a truly hideous purple beverage. If you put a Fizzy directly onto your tongue, your mouth would spew purple foam and you would look like some kind of sick young alien being. Looking back on our diet, I'm frankly surprised that we considered the hydrogen bomb such a big threat.

Speaking of dieting: 1950 was historic in that it was the year when The World's Most Beautiful Woman, Elizabeth Taylor, age 18, got married for the very first time, to one of the nation's most eligible bachelors: Buffalo Bob.

No, it wasn't Buffalo Bob. It was some guy, and I'd look up his name, but I figure he's going to be out of the picture by the time we get to . . .

1951

This was the year that the world truly entered the Computer Age, as the first general-purpose commercial computer, UNIVAC, went into service for the Census Bureau. That original computer was retired in 1963, and now passes the time playing solitaire in a condominium on Miami Beach and mailing incorrect credit-card statements to consumers selected at random.

In another 1951 development, Earl Tupper began selling the plastic resealable food containers that would make his name famous: Earlware.

No, seriously, it was Tupperware, and it went on to become a big marketing success, thanks to the concept of Tupperware Parties, where the housewives of the Fifties would get together at somebody's house not only to buy food containers, but also to chat, play party games, and light up reefers the size of highway flares.

No, that probably isn't true, either. But the housewives of the Fifties definitely could have used some kind of stress relief. Back then, women generally stayed home, which was both good and bad: good, in the sense that they spent a lot of time with their children; bad, in the sense that they spent a lot of time with their children. Small children are a never-ending source of joy and happiness for about fifteen minutes, after which they can really get on your nerves, especially if their blood content is 74 percent Bosco.

I know that in the Fifties I, personally, exchanged at least 275 million punches with my sister and/or brothers in the backseat of the car when my mom was driving us to Brownies or Boy Scouts or Little League or grocery shopping or any of the countless other errands she had to run while my dad, like everybody else's dad, was off somewhere wearing a suit and having a career. And for every one of those 275 million punches, my mom—this was her job—had to turn halfway around in her seat and say "Stop it!" This had the same deterrent effect on us as a gnat has on a freight locomotive.

A few years ago, a woman I know, about my age, told me about a memory she had from her childhood—a vivid memory of her mom, more than once, standing out in the backyard, hanging diapers on the line to dry, and weeping. At the time, my friend didn't understand this behavior, but later, when she became a mother herself, she figured that her mom was experiencing the sense of despair that sometimes overcomes a mother whose life is severely restricted by the needs and demands of small children. Today, of course, many more women have careers outside the home, which means they get to experience the sense of despair that sometimes overcomes a mother who must spend long periods of time separated from her young children.

It is SO much easier to be a guy.

There was one woman in 1951 who never seemed at all restricted: This was Lucille Ball, star of the new show *I Love Lucy*, which became hugely popular because it explored the theme of the angst caused by the rootlessness and quest for meaning among the emerging American middle class.

I am joking, of course. It became popular because it explored the theme of whether Lucy and Ethel could get away with dressing up as men and trying to sneak into Ricky's and Fred's golf tournament. I watched *I Love Lucy*, but I was more into another show that debuted in 1951: *Roy Rogers*, featuring Roy and his wife, Dale; his horse, Trigger; her horse, Buttermilk; their dog, Bullet; the comical sidekick, Pat Brady; and Pat's comical Jeep, Nellybelle. This show is not to be confused with *The Adventures of Wild Bill Hickok,* where there was no wife or Jeep or dog, the comical sidekick was Jingles, and the horse was Buckshot; nor with *The Cisco Kid,* where the comical sidekick was Pancho and the horse was named—you guessed it—Buffalo Bob.

No, the truth—and I am ashamed of this—is that I can't remember the name of the Cisco Kid's horse. But I do remember another 1951 show, *Watch Mr. Wizard,* in which Mr. Wizard conducted amazing yet educational scientific experiments. For example, I remember one episode where he showed how you could, by using vinegar and baking soda, cause a hard-boiled egg to get sucked into a milk bottle; this demonstrated the scientific principle that Mr. Wizard had way more spare time than anybody else.

Mr. Wizard also once did an experiment with a vacuum cleaner and a Ping-Pong ball; this taught me the scientific principle that if you plugged the vacuum-cleaner hose into the *other* end of the vacuum cleaner, it would blow instead of suck, and if you attempted to use this principle to create a miniature hurricane involving the bathtub, your mom would get very upset.

Speaking of scientific advances, in 1951 the Chrysler Corporation began offering power steering in some car models. Back then cars had power nothing and manual everything. These were big, squatting hulks of steel with running boards and hood ornaments and massive fenders and backseats large enough to transport cattle in, where kids, unfettered by seat belts or car seats or any other safety device, had plenty of room to roam and punch each other.

People were more *involved* with their cars back then. They had to be. You sometimes hear older people complain about modern cars, saying, "They don't build 'em like they used to." I'm here to tell you that this is a good thing, because the way they used to build 'em, at least one tire would go flat every 75 feet. I cannot count the number of times I sat by the side of the road, watching my dad, or somebody else's dad, putting the jack under the bumper and jacking up the car, or occasionally just jacking up the bumper, leaving the rest of the car still squatting on the ground, because they used to build 'em in such a way that the bumpers sometimes came off.

Cars in those days were also always "flooding." To this day I'm not clear on what "flooding" means, but it happened all the time to us. The car wouldn't start, and Dad would open the hood, look at the engine, frown, and announce: "It's flooded." We didn't know what "it" was, but we did know that it meant we weren't going anywhere for a while, and that if "it" continued to be "flooded," our battery—one of the most fragile mechanisms on the face of the earth—would run down, and we might catch Dad saying a bad word.

Speaking of bad words: Many of them were uttered in the fall of 1951 by Brooklyn residents when Bobby Thomson hit the bottom-of-the-ninth home run to beat the Dodgers and give the Giants the National League pennant. That same year the Giants signed Willie Mays, and the Yankees signed Mickey Mantle; these men would become the biggest stars in what was, in the 1950s, America's only *real* big-league sport.

We Boomer boys grew up immersed in baseball: We collected cards; we listened to games on the radio; we carried our gloves everywhere and played every chance we got. If we had to, we could play baseball with a total of three players, which is fifteen players short of the officially recommended total. If there were only two of us, we played catch, hour after hour, until it got so dark that we had to throw the ball high, so the other guy could see it against the stars. If there was nobody else around, we played catch against a wall.

I very rarely see kids playing catch anymore; I don't think my son even owns a baseball glove. He and his friends prefer sports such as basketball, football, and hassling people on the Internet. I, too, have pretty much lost interest in baseball. I'm not sure why: Either baseball got more boring, or I have lost the ability to become absorbed in the subtle strategic intricacies of a sport that seems to consist mainly of standing around. But I was *nuts* for baseball in the 1950s, and I have to say that playing and following the sport taught me two important principles that have guided me throughout my life:

1. There is a very, very good reason why male baseball players wear protective cups.
2. The New York Yankees are evil.

As it happens, the Yankees won the 1951 World Series, so it wasn't an entirely good year. But it did see the birth of a product that, years later, would make my life a lot easier: In 1951, the disposable diaper was invented by Marion Donovan. A mom.

1952

This was the year that historians refer to as The Year of Bald Guys Running for President: Dwight Eisenhower vs. Adlai Stevenson. My parents were Democrats; they put a STEVENSON sticker on our car bumper, to persuade voters who drove past us while we were waiting by the side of the road for our car to stop being "flooded."

Despite my parents' efforts, the voters chose Eisenhower and his comical sidekick, Dick Nixon, who got into a scandal and was in danger of being kicked off the ticket until he saved himself by giving his famous "Checkers Speech," so called because Nixon talked about his family's cocker spaniel, Buffalo Bob.[3]

For many of us Boomers, Eisenhower is the first president we can really remember; he was the Nation's Grandfather, an old guy off somewhere being in charge of the government, whatever *that* was. Of far more importance to us (some of us, anyway) was a magazine that was first published in 1952: *Mad*. I *loved Mad*. It was so . . . so . . . *subversive*. *Mad* looked at America—its people, its politics, its businesses, its schools, its movies, its music, its TV shows—and *Mad* said: "Hey, this is *stupid*." This became the fundamental underlying premise of Boomer humor, epitomized by the glory years of *Saturday Night Live*.

Speaking of shows that did not require a degree in rocket science to comprehend, 1952 was the television debut season

---

3. We regret to inform you that this will be the last Buffalo Bob joke.

of *The Adventures of Ozzie and Harriet*, which ran for more than ten years with the same five-element plot:

ELEMENT 1: Something happens.
ELEMENT 2: Ozzie doesn't understand it.
ELEMENT 3: So Harriet explains it to him.
ELEMENT 4: So there's a happy ending.
ELEMENT 5: But Ozzie still doesn't really understand it.

Ozzie, bumbling and frowning his way cluelessly around the house, personified an important theme in American popular culture: the theme that the average adult male is an idiot. I don't know why this theme is so popular, and neither do the other adult males I know. But it ticks us off and makes us want to blow stuff up.

Two other popular TV shows that appeared in 1952 were *My Little Margie* and *Our Miss Brooks.* These shows are easily confused because they both featured actors named "Gale." So to make sure that this important cultural information is passed along correctly to future generations, I have prepared this reference table:

ACTORS NAMED GALE
IN SITUATION COMEDIES DEBUTING IN 1952

NAME OF SHOW	LAST NAME OF GALE	GENDER OF GALE
My Little Margie	Storm	Female
Our Miss Brooks	Gordon	Male

Keep this information in a safe place, future generations! This is our legacy to you!

Dragnet also came out in 1952 and was a hit despite not having anybody in it named Gale. It did have a catchy musical theme (all together: "BOM, BA-BOM BOMP") and it starred Jack Webb as Detective Joe Friday, who, assisted by his side-kick,[4] fought crime by driving around Los Angeles displaying the same range of facial expressions as a sea urchin. Which reminds me that 1952 was also the year of the coronation of Queen Elizabeth II.

But the *most* important thing that happened in 1952, if you were a kid, was the development, by Jonas Salk, of a vaccine for polio, which was then an epidemic. Kids my age were too young to really understand what polio was, but we definitely picked up on the fact that it was a bad thing that our parents worried about a lot. I knew that, whatever it was, some of my parents' friends' children had gotten it, and that my mom, even though she tried to hide it, got very upset when my sister or I got sick.

I know now that Dr. Salk's vaccine was a wonderful discovery that spared many families from tragedy. But that is *not* how I felt about it in the early 1950s. To me, all the Salk vaccine represented was: shots. One day, I was a carefree child with nothing more important on my mind than what I was going to be next Halloween,[5] and the next day I found myself standing in a line of kids in the Wampus School cafeteria waiting for Dr.

---

4. I don't remember his name, but he was *not* comical.
5. Batman.

Cohn—Dr. Cohn! Who delivered me! Who always seemed like such a nice man!—to *stick a needle into my arm.*

The grown-ups told us that this was good for us, but many of us were extremely doubtful. As I say, we were vague on the concept of polio, but we couldn't imagine that it would be worse than having somebody stick an actual needle into your arm. Some of us, when we got to the front of the line, struggled and cried and had to be held firmly in position by a large and powerful nurse.

"It won't hurt!" she kept telling us.

I did not believe her for one second. I was confident that if Dr. Cohn had tried to stick the needle into *her* arm, she'd have stuffed him into the dishwasher.

Despite my struggling, I got through my polio shots, and now of course I'm glad I did. But the shots *did* hurt. The lesson that a lot of Boomers learned from this experience was this: Grown-ups, sometimes with the best of intentions, will look you right in the eye and lie. And they hadn't even *started* talking to us about drugs.

1953

In 1953 the Russians got their hydrogen bomb, thereby tying the arms race at two big scary weapons per side. This left the United States with no choice but to start developing ballistic missiles, thus forcing the Russians to develop ballistic missiles, thus forcing us to develop *anti*-ballistic missiles, and so on for the next forty years, with each side producing increasingly sophisticated (by which I mean "expensive") weapons, culminating in the Amazing Invisible "Stealth" Bomber, which is so sophisticated that its commode alone costs more than the entire annual educational budget of New Jersey,[6] and which I believe we are still building, or at least spending money on, despite the fact that the Soviet Union collapsed some years ago and the entire Russian industrial apparatus is currently devoted to making fake Rolex watches.

Elsewhere abroad in 1953, the British explorer Edmund Hillary was hailed as a hero when he became the first man to climb Mount Everest, although he acknowledged that he never would have made it without his skilled and courageous Sherpa guide, Buffalo Bob.[7]

On the domestic front, Americans were hearing and seeing the first stirrings of the youthful craziness that would soon sweep the nation. The record charts were still dominated by songs like Patti Page's "How Much Is That Doggie in the Window?"[8] but a group called Bill Haley and The Comets also came out with the song "Crazy Man, Crazy," whose title exemplified the "cool" new "lingo" used by "hep cats" who were "digging" a "groovy" new sound called "Rock 'n' Roll," which would soon have the whole country "jiving" and putting everything in "quotation marks."

Yes, youthful rebellion was in the air, and nobody personified it better than Marlon Brando, who in those days was young and handsome and slim enough to wear a leather jacket

---

6. This is because it's an invisible commode (which makes it very difficult to hit).
7. So I lied.
8. Which was also a huge hit for Metallica.

made from only one cow. In 1953 he starred in the movie *The Wild One,* about a town being terrorized by a motorcycle gang (in those days motorcycle gangs consisted of defiant outcasts; today, of course, they tend to be orthodontists).

Speaking of rebels: In 1953, 27-year-old Hugh Hefner, courageously defying the repressed, restrictive "button-down" middle-class moral climate of the times, published the first issue of *Playboy* magazine, which dared to make the sophisticated intellectual statement: "Take a gander at these bazooms!"

Playboy was to become a *major* factor in the development of millions of Boomer boys. Most of us knew somebody whose older brother or dad or uncle had a stack of old *Playboys* somewhere, and we spent countless hours reading them. Well, okay, we weren't actually *reading* them, but we were definitely *absorbing* them, because they were the only source of information that we considered absolutely vital: namely, what women looked like naked.

The only other reliable source of this type of information during my youth was *National Geographic,* which was always doing pictorial features on various different primitive tribes wherein the women went topless. Either that, or it was always the *same* primitive tribe, and *National Geographic,* in a shrewd circulation-boosting move, just kept printing pictures of it under different names. But whatever the explanation, when a new issue of *National Geographic* used to arrive in the library of the Harold C. Crittenden Junior High School, it was immediately analyzed for breast content, and this information was rapidly disseminated throughout the school ("Nipple on page 137!"), whereupon the entire male student population would descend on the library and display a sudden passionate interest in geography.

Speaking of passion: In 1953, John F. Kennedy married Jacqueline Lee Bouvier, although this reportedly had little effect on his social life.

On the sports scene, the Boston Braves baseball team moved to Milwaukee. That was big news, because in those days professional teams rarely moved. Today, professional teams—especially football teams—change cities so often that only powerful computers can keep track of them ("In sports today, the Phoenix Cardinals, who used to be the St. Louis Cardinals, took a seemingly insurmountable three-touchdown lead into the fourth quarter of their game against the Indianapolis Colts, who used to be the Baltimore Colts—not to be confused with the Baltimore Ravens, who used to be the Cleveland Browns—only to see the game slip from their grasp when, with three seconds left in the game, the Colts announced that they were moving to Albuquerque to become a professional ice hockey team called the New Mexico Sand Particles").

For TV viewers, 1953 brought good news and bad news:

- The good news was that the networks started broadcasting some shows in color.
- The bad news was that these colors did not resemble anything on the immediate planet.

I don't know what the problem was,[9] but on the color TV sets of that era, you could *never* get the picture to look natural.

---

9. Maybe the TV sets were "flooded."

This was especially true of human skin: No matter how much you fiddled with the knobs, people on TV always came out either green or bright orange, so that everybody looked like either Kermit the Frog or The Human Cheez-It.

Of course most of us didn't have color TVs. But we were happy with our black and white sets, watching new 1953 shows such as *Superman,* starring George Reeves as the Man of Steel and the mild-mannered reporter Clark Kent, who never wrote any stories because he was too busy ducking into phone booths to change into his Superman outfit (Clark apparently believed that nobody could see him inside a phone booth). I loved *Superman,* and, like many kids of that era, I spent a lot of time running around the house with my arms out in front of me, my cape—made from a towel pinned around my neck—fluttering out behind. Perhaps this is why, when it came time to have a career, I entered Clark's field, journalism. Of course, when I found out that journalists were expected to actually *work,* I decided to become a humor writer, which is a far less restrictive profession. Although sometimes I get a rash from my neck towel.

1954

Some seriously major events occurred in 1954.

First, the French got their butts kicked in Vietnam, which had become a hellhole quagmire, a totally unnecessary disaster, a towering example of national stupidity and arrogance bordering on the criminally insane. The reaction of U.S.

foreign-policy thinkers was: "Hey! WE need to get involved in that!"

Our thinkers reacted that way because of the Domino Theory, which was very popular at the time. This theory held that if we let godless Communism topple Vietnam, it would then topple Cambodia, which would in turn topple Thailand, which would in turn topple whatever country is next to Thailand, which would in turn topple the Pacific Ocean, and so on until downtown Muncie, Indiana, was overrun with godless Communists, setting fire to churches and opening Thai restaurants that served spicy and godless foods.

The Domino Theory turned out to be uncannily accurate, except for one teensy flaw, which was that it was all wrong. The Communists eventually did take over Vietnam, but instead of godlessness, they wound up exporting $140-per-pair Nike footwear (which, you could argue, is worse).

But back in 1954, the Domino Theory was all the rage. So when the French gave up in Vietnam, the United States began quietly stepping in. Most American citizens paid no attention; they were busy adjusting the knobs on their new TV sets.

The second major event in 1954 was that the U.S. Supreme Court ruled that segregated public schools were illegal, thereby starting the civil rights revolution, which ultimately resulted in the universal racial harmony that we enjoy today.

I am of course kidding again. We are as close to enjoying universal racial harmony as the Unabomber is to serving on the Supreme Court. But we've definitely made progress. We older Baby Boomers spent our early years in a society that was rigidly segregated. I remember family-vacation car trips from

New York to Florida in the 1950s; as we passed through the South, stopping frequently so my father could repair flat tires, we'd see "WHITE" and "COLORED" signs on bathrooms and water fountains. My sister and I knew that this was wrong (our dad told us) and sometimes, after looking around to make sure nobody was watching, we drank from the "COLORED" fountains, thus striking a bold blow for equality that I'm sure played a vital role in bringing the white power structure to its knees.

There was one area in which integration was definitely making progress in 1954: music. Rock 'n' Roll Fever was building among American teenagers, and they were not satisfied with the songs coming from the white music industry, which was pushing such young stars as Eddie Fisher singing "Oh! My Papa."

So white kids started listening to the musicians that black people were listening to—people like Muddy Waters, the Drifters, and Fats Domino Theory. What the kids discovered was that there was a Coolness Gap between the white and black cultures, with the black culture way ahead. The desire to imitate black culture—to close the Coolness Gap by listening to black music, learning black dances, talking and acting "black"— became another defining characteristic of the Boomers, many of whom still, at age 50, will celebrate successful lease negotiations by exchanging high fives.

The wave of young white singers who began emerging in 1954 owed much of their sound to black music. The ultimate example, of course, was a shy 19-year-old truck driver who in July of that year walked into the Sun recording studio in

Memphis and made his first record—"That's All Right" and "Blue Moon of Kentucky"—thus beginning what would become one of the most amazing careers in entertainment history. That young man, needless to say, was: Buffalo Bob.

On the medical front, researchers in 1954 were finding more and more evidence that smoking causes lung cancer, but this news didn't put much of a dent in America's cigarette consumption. Back then, it seemed as though all the grown-ups smoked all the time. Every office, waiting room, bus, train, and theater was filled with a blue haze; cigarettes were advertised relentlessly on TV by attractive actors who seemed to be achieving supreme happiness and fulfillment from sucking on burning tobacco wads.

Our parents responded to the medical news by telling us kids, between inhales, that we should not smoke. Their flagrant hypocrisy about cigarettes, combined with the way they lied to us about the polio shots, caused us kids to start developing serious doubts about the wisdom of our elders. I mean, these people liked *Eddie Fisher.*

I'll tell you a person we kids did admire in 1954: Davy Crockett. His story was featured on the new TV show *Disneyland,* and he instantly became the hugest and most important historical figure of all time, at least as far as the second-grade boys at Wampus Elementary School were concerned. We *loved* Davy Crockett, and every day at recess we reenacted his heroic last stand against the Mexican army at the Alamo, with the playground slide playing the part of the Alamo, about thirty-four of us boys playing the part of Davy Crockett, and virtually nobody playing the part of the Mexican army. (These were not historically accurate reenactments; the Davy Crocketts always kicked butt.)

My mom got me a Davy Crockett T-shirt, which I wore for about 400 days in a row. I cannot remember any of the sonnets of Shakespeare, but I can remember several verses of "The Ballad of Davy Crockett," starting with:

> *Born on a mountaintop in Tennessee*
> *Greenest state in the land of the free*
> *Raised in the woods so he knew every tree*
> *Kilt him a b'ar, when he was only three*
> *Davy, Davy Crockett!*
> *King of the wild frontier!*

In 1954 I saw my first Really Major Motion Picture, *20,000 Leagues Under the Sea.* This was the *Star Wars* of 1954. My dad took me to see it at New York's Radio City Music Hall, where we had to stand in line for hours. But it was worth it for me because of the scene where the occupants of Captain Nemo's submarine, the *Nautilus,* are attacked by the tentacles of a giant squid, representing state-of-the-art 1954 special effects. I was thrilled and terrified, although today that scene looks like men pretending to wrestle a fire hose.

On TV, two of the popular new shows were dog-related: *Rin Tin Tin* and *Lassie.* Both of these shows were based on the comically inaccurate premise that dogs are intelligent. *Lassie,* in my opinion, is the least realistic television program ever made. I mean, here you had this *brilliant* dog, living with the world's stupidest farm family. These people were so stupid that they hardly ever left the house. They just sat around the kitchen all day, looking out the window and wondering: "How come all the neighbors have *crops?*"

And it was a good thing that they didn't leave the house, because when they did, they inevitably got into some life-threatening situation. Dad would get trapped under his tractor, or young Jeff—who later became young Timmy, and these people were so stupid that they didn't even notice *that*—would get trapped by quicksand. (And just who the hell buys a farm with quicksand on it?)

So Lassie would go racing back to the kitchen and scratch at the door and bark and whimper, and even though this happened *every single week*, this moronic family would never realize that Jeff/Timmy was in trouble.

"What's wrong, girl?" they'd ask. "Are you hungry?"

Now a *real* dog would go, "Hell yes! I'm hungry!" A real dog would go in and eat and spend the rest of the evening licking its private parts and forget all about Jeff/Timmy.

But not Lassie. Lassie would keep scratching and barking and whimpering until finally even these people figured out what was going on, and they'd go rescue Jeff/Timmy, and the episode would end happily with the reunited Moron Family sitting around the dining-room table, and Lassie filling out the agricultural-subsidy forms.

Speaking of non–rocket scientist TV families: 1954 also saw the debut of *Father Knows Best*. This popular sitcom starred Jane Wyatt as the cheerful mom and Robert Young as the father who was so relentlessly genial that you suspected that during the commercials he was sneaking down to the basement and inhaling from a humongous bong.

To help Americans remain overweight while they watched TV, Swanson came out with a breakthrough product in 1954: The Frozen TV Dinner. Now, for the first time, consumers could have the convenience of enjoying, in one convenient tray, a vegetable, a meatlike substance, and a dessert, all heated to exactly the same temperature, and all tasting exactly alike. (I don't know how they make TV dinners, but I've always pictured a huge, frigid warehouse where burly men use chain saws to cut individual servings off mountainous frozen lumps of gray stuff labeled with big signs that say things like "MASHED POTATOES" and "MEAT LOAF OR POSSIBLY APPLE COBBLER.")

Yes, 1954 brought some glorious improvements for humanity, but it was not a year unmarred by tragedy. I refer specifically—as you have no doubt guessed—to the death of Dr. Samuel J. Crumbine, the man who, in 1905, invented the flyswatter.

1955

In 1955 Nikita Khrushchev became the head honcho in the Soviet Union. He was bald and had a kind of warty thing growing on his face, so we knew he was godless. Meanwhile, our bald but godly leader, Dwight Eisenhower, had a heart attack, and for a little while there was some concern that Dick Nixon would have to take over Eisenhower's presidential activities.

This would have been scary because these activities consisted mainly of golfing, and God only knows how many innocent bystanders Dick might have killed if he had been permitted to swing a nine iron.

Fortunately, Ike recovered quickly. The same could not be said for two other famous men who died in 1955:

• Albert Einstein, who discovered that a tiny amount of mass is equal to a huge amount of energy, which explains why, as Einstein himself so eloquently put it in a famous 1939 speech to the Physics Department at Princeton: "You have to exercise for a week to work off the thigh fat from a single Snickers."

• Oscar Mayer, who was a real person and whose groundbreaking work in the field of meat ultimately led to one of history's most significant technological advances, the Weinermobile.

On the business front, by 1955 the United States was being flooded with cheap, shoddy products from Japan. We of course laughed at these products and at the Japanese; we could not imagine in our wildest dreams that they would one day stomp on our consumer-electronics industry the way Godzilla stomped on Tokyo. If somebody had told us that the Japanese would eventually try to sell us *cars*, we would have laughed and laughed, and then we would have gone back to trying to start our flooded Nash Ramblers.

In aviation, the most significant development was the completion of Chicago's O'Hare Airport. It officially began operations with United Airlines Flight No. 325, which was scheduled to fly to Denver, although as of late 1997 it had not received clearance to take off.

For us Boomers, the big event of 1955 was the opening of Disneyland, named for its creator, one of the most successful and visionary entertainment entrepreneurs in history: Donald Trump.[10]

Disneyland was more than just an amusement park: It was an amusement park with really *enormous* waiting lines. Americans loved Disneyland, because it gave them something good, something decent, something that epitomized a quality that vacationing American families value above all else: clean toilets.

Before Disneyland, Americans were forced to settle for vacation destinations such as the outdoors, or historic sites, or cities, or even foreign countries, all of which tended to have poor restroom facilities, and some of which also contained foreigners. But at Disneyland, a family could enjoy a totally hygienic restroom environment, plus they could eat regular, safe American food such as french fries, yet they could still experience the excitement of visiting, for example, a simulated African jungle river, where they could board a simulated boat and take a ride past simulated rocks and simulated wild animals that would suddenly pop up and give the family a nice little simulated scare without eating anybody or pooping or having sex or any of the other gross things that non-theme-park nature is always doing. And then the family, still chewing their fries, could walk a short distance and learn about simu-

---

10. You thought I was going to say Buffalo Bob.

lated history by watching a robot that looked like Abraham Lincoln deliver the Gettysburg Address exactly as the real Abraham Lincoln would have delivered it had he been a robot.

When we Boomers weren't nagging our parents to please please PLEASE take us to Disneyland, we were tuning in to the hot new 1955 kids' show, *The Mickey Mouse Club*, which featured a bunch of kids who were just like us except they had talent, which they displayed on the Talent Roundup. I was deeply envious of the Mousketeers, and I would have done anything to be declared an Honorary Mousketeer ("Step right up! Here's your ears!") except that I didn't have any talent, unless you counted the ability, picked up on the mean playground of Wampus Elementary, to make a farting noise with my armpit.

So like most kids, I had to settle for admiring the Mouske-teers from afar, especially Annette, who stirred vague unex-plained yearnings in many young males during the 1950s when she came out for the Mousketeer Roll Call and proudly revealed her name printed across the front of her T-shirt. We definitely scrutinized Annette's name more carefully than, for example, Cubby's.

Other important shows appearing on TV in 1955 were *Andy's Gang*, which was significant because it gave humanity the amazingly useful phrase "Plunk your magic twanger, Froggy!"; and the adventure show *Robin Hood*, which was sig-nificant because for more than forty years now its theme song has been playing in my brain:

Robin Hood, Robin Hood, riding through the glen!
Robin Hood, Robin Hood, with his band of men!

Feared by the bad! Loved by the good!
Robin Hood! Robin Hood! Robin Hood!

But for Boomers, probably the most influential new TV personality to appear in 1955 was Captain Kangaroo.[11] He was calm and gentle, and we kids trusted him absolutely. I think we still do. In fact, it amazes me that neither major political party has had the brains to nominate Captain Kangaroo for president, because he'd win in a landslide. I mean, think of the presidents we've had in your lifetime; do you really believe that Captain Kangaroo—or, for that matter, Mister Green Jeans—could possibly have done any worse? Me either.

Speaking of jeans: In 1955 young Americans started wearing them, inspired by trend-setting hepcat studs Marlon Brando in *The Wild One* and James Dean in *Rebel Without a Cause*. It's hard to imagine this today, when everybody except the Pope wears jeans to everything including funerals, but in the Fifties they were generally considered a low-class form of attire suitable mainly for your pig farmer. We were NOT allowed to wear jeans to school. We boys had to wear "khakis," a.k.a. "chinos," a.k.a. Dork Pants. We hated these pants then, although when we reached middle age we made them hugely popular once again under the brand name Dockers, which was chosen because it sounds better than "Pants for the Bigger-Butted Man."

Elvis Presley, who did not have a big butt in 1955, was rapidly changing status from Total Nobody to Planetary Heart-

---

11. **Real name: Lieutenant Kangaroo.**

throb, and "Rock Around the Clock," by Bill Haley and The Comets, was a hit record. Rock and roll was definitely winning the hearts and minds of us younger people, and our parents' generation (which was tapping its feet to Lawrence Welk's new TV show) could not decide whether it was just a passing fad or a godless Communist plot. As if the Communists could *ever* come up with lyrics like "You ain't never caught a rabbit, and you ain't no friend of mine."

1956

This was a presidential election year, and the Democrats, having learned a harsh lesson from the beating that Adlai Stevenson took in 1952, shrewdly responded by nominating: Adlai Stevenson. For vice president, they nominated Senator Estes Kefauver. The big selling point for this ticket was that if, God forbid, something were to happen to Adlai, the nation would still be led by a person with a comical name.

But despite the strong support of both my parents and maybe fourteen other voters, the Democrat ticket once again lost to Dwight and Dick. The big achievement of the second Eisenhower administration was the federal interstate highway system, which would revolutionize American life by enabling residents of many out-of-the-way rural communities to experience something that their ancestors did not even dream of: carsickness.

As the interstate system has stretched across the country, it has made automotive travel much more convenient, but it has also destroyed what was a major component of family vacation travel in my childhood: roadside attractions. Back when there were no superhighways, tourists traveled on smaller local roads, and we were always encountering signs like this:

> **SEE THE WORLD'S**
> **LARGEST**
> **CEMENT HARMONICA!**
> **JUST 53 MILES ON LEFT**

Of course we'd nag our parents strenuously for the entire fifty-three miles to please please PLEASE stop and let us see the attraction, which always turned out to be some pathetically unimpressive thing that had been acquiring grime since 1923. We'd stand around with the other tourists and stare at it, cowlike, for a few minutes; then we'd get back into the car and drive for a few more miles, until we saw a sign that said something like this:

> **APHID VILLAGE**
> **ONLY 97 MILES!**

Which was our cue to start begging again.

You don't see roadside attractions on the interstate; you just see the interstate, punctuated by the occasional exit, where there will be (this is federal law) a Days Inn motel, a Speedway gas station, a McDonald's, a Wendy's, a Hardee's, a Burger King, a Waffle House, and a Stuckey's. "No Matter Where You Go, It's The Same Place" is the official interstate motto. I think it would be nice if the federal government constructed new roadside attractions at some of the exits, so that after you got your fill-up at the Speedway, you could chew your Stuckey's pecan log while admiring, say, a scale model of the Battle of Gettysburg made entirely from seaweed. I think that would be at least as good a use for our taxes as the Department of Agriculture.

Another 1956 development that would have a major impact on the American way of life was the completion of the first enclosed shopping mall. It's difficult to imagine now, but back in the pre-mall era, shoppers had to physically go outdoors to get from one store to another, and there were some communities that—prepare to be stunned—*did not have a Gap*. Many stores in those days were owned by individual humans. For example, in Armonk, we had the grocery store, which was owned by Mr. Briccetti; the drugstore, which was owned by Mr. DiGiacinto; Louie the cleaner's, which was owned by Louie the Cleaner; and the Armonk Stationery Store, which we called "Art's" because it was owned by Art, who sold cigarettes and candy but not stationery. When you walked into these stores, the owners were always there, and they knew you by name, and if you happened not to have enough money on you for an urgent medical requirement such as a Three Musketeers bar, they'd let you have it anyway, because they knew your folks would pay for it next time they came in. Just like Wal-Mart!

On the cultural front, 1956 was the year of the first Godzilla movie, which launched the golden age of Japanese monster movies. Sure, the plots were absurd and the acting was terrible, but there was no denying the fact that the special effects were also extremely bad. Still, these movies taught us an important moral lesson that is worth bearing in mind today: If the human race, in its careless arrogance, disturbs the natural order of the universe, then gigantic radioactive lobsters will come and knock over the human race's commuter trains.

Speaking of gigantic: Elvis became absolutely huge in 1956, selling zillions of copies of "Hound Dog," "Don't Be Cruel," and "Heartbreak Hotel," not to mention "Love Me Tender," which, even when it was played on the extremely low-fidelity record player at my sister's eleventh birthday party (this made a big impression on me) caused the girls to whimper. Other rockers with big hits that year were Chuck Berry, singing "Roll Over, Beethoven," Fats Domino[12] singing "Blueberry Hill," Carl Perkins singing "Blue Suede Shoes," and of course Perry "Soul Man" Como singing "Hot Diggity (Dog Ziggity Boom)."

The hot new TV show was *To Tell the Truth,* on which a panel of celebrities tried to figure out which contestant really was who he or she claimed to be ("Will the real Hunchback of Notre Dame please stand up!"). The hot new advertising jingle— which, even though I never used the product, has remained firmly lodged in my memory ever since, and which will proba- bly be the last thing to go through my brain when I die—was "You'll wonder where the yellow went, when you brush your teeth with Pepsodent!"

In 1956 foreign affairs, the Communist Russians sent their

---

12. In later years, yielding to the pressure of political correctness, he changed his name to "Person of Size Domino."

godless tanks into Hungary to squash the Hungarian rebellion, an event that had a direct impact on Armonk in the form of the arrival of a Hungarian refugee family, the Deaks, which included three boys who could play soccer but not baseball, which we thought was really weird. Also there was the Suez Crisis, which was historically very significant, although to be honest I've never really been clear on exactly where, or what, the "Suez" is, and now that I'm 50, I say the hell with it.

1957

There was big trouble this year for the Boomers. There we were, innocently enjoying our childhoods, when, without warning, the Russians launched the first man-made, Earth-orbiting godless satellite, named *Sputnik*.[13] America went *crazy*. Until then, we had assumed that we were far superior to the Russians, because they were just a bunch of vodka-swilling potato chompers wearing bad suits, whereas we were a highly advanced consumer society with color televisions and Amana freezers and record players with as many as four speeds. And suddenly we find out that the Russians were BEATING US IN THE SPACE RACE!!!

Guess who got punished for this. Do you think it was the grown-ups, who *let* the Russians get ahead? Of course not. It was the same group that had to get the polio shots: us kids. All kinds of experts came crawling out of the academic woodwork

---

13. This is a Russian word meaning "sound of a person sneezing."

to declare that American students were science and math morons, frittering away our brainpower playing Davy Crockett while Russian children were learning about the cosine.

And so I remember 1957 as the year when school became less fun. From that point on, we spent a lot less time making authentic medieval castles out of papier-mâché, and a lot more time learning about the ionosphere. I suppose this change also had to do with the fact that we were getting older, but at the time I viewed it as yet another reason to hate the Russians.

The great irony is that while everybody was obsessing over *Sputnik,* an American company was coming out with an innovative aeronautical advance that was WAY cooler than some beeping basketball in space. I refer to the Wham-O Corporation, which in 1957 gave the world the Frisbee, a product that has provided billions of hours of high-quality entertainment to several generations of humans and several dozen generations of dogs.

Speaking of entertainment: 1957 brought some fine new TV programs, including *Leave It to Beaver,* which will stand forever as a symbol of an age so innocent that there could be a TV show featuring a main character called "The Beaver"; and *Perry Mason,* which was about a defense attorney who had the good fortune to be practicing law in a community whose residents were so stupid they made the family on *Lassie* look like rocket scientists. There was one murder per week in this community, so you'd think that, under the law of averages, the law-enforcement authorities, led by District Attorney Hamilton Burger, would at least occasionally arrest a guilty person. But they *never* did. They *always* arrested an innocent person, and that person *always* hired Perry Mason, who *always* won the case, because it turned out that the criminals in this community were even stupider than the law-enforcement authorities: In the middle of one of Perry's cross-examinations, the guilty person would *always* jump up, right in court, and confess to the murder. So basically all Perry had to do was send out bills, although this part was never shown on the show.

But for us kids, the important new show of 1957 was *American Bandstand,* starring Dick Clark[14] as himself, along with a cast of actual live teenagers ("Mary, 16, South Philly") who rated the new records ("It has a good beat; I give it an 8") and did hot new dances such as the Stroll and the Slop. Kids watched the show religiously, dancing along to the music, the whole young American nation learning to Stroll in unison while Russian kids studied algebra. We didn't care: We were now totally into rock and roll, and we were buying records like crazy—not just Elvis records, but also songs like "Bye Bye Love" by the Everly Brothers; "Diana"[15] by Paul Anka; "That'll Be the Day" by Buddy Holly and the Crickets (that was the first record I ever bought); "You Send Me" by Sam Cooke; and of course "Round and Round" by Perry "Mojo" Como.

On the commercial front, Crest toothpaste, seeking to create a commercial concept even more annoying than "You'll wonder where the yellow went, when you brush your teeth with Pepsodent!" hit the jackpot with "Look Mom—no cavities!" The slogan was aimed at Mom because of course Dad was not

---

14. **Current estimated age: 147.**
15. **"I'm so young and you're so old; this my darling I've been told."**

home; Dad was at work, conducting serious business and drinking serious martinis with fellow suit-wearing executives of Amalgamated Consolidated Conglomerated Coagulated Corporation. Dad was busy earning money so that the family could purchase the new Buick, which boasted *44 pounds* of chromed trim. The Russians may have had working space satellites, but they had nothing like *that*.

1958

If I had to pick one year to represent the Fifties, I'd pick 1958. For one thing, it was the year that the folks at Wham-O, always looking for new ways to raise the level of American culture, gave us the Hula Hoop. This was a bright-colored plastic hoop that you spun around your hips using a hula-type motion. I realize that this sounds stupid, but you must trust me when I tell you, as one who participated extensively in this fad, that it really *was* stupid. In terms of intellectual content, the Hula Hoop made the Frisbee look like international championship chess.

Speaking of mindlessness, another reason why I believe 1958 epitomized the 1950s was that it was the Year of the Hugely Popular Truly Dumb Novelty Record. Among the big hits were "The Purple People Eater" and "The Witch Doctor." (Everybody join in: "Oo, ee, oo ah ah, ting, tang, walla walla bing bang." Okay! Now everybody, try to get that out of your head!) Among the hot new recording sensations were The Chipmunks, which was supposedly a group of singing chipmunks. (They weren't *really* chipmunks, of course; they were young squirrels.)

I'm happy to note that there were also some serious and important songs produced in 1958, including "At the Hop" by Danny and the Juniors, "Great Balls of Fire" by Jerry Lee Lewis, "Yakety Yak" by the Coasters, and "Catch a Falling Star" by Perry "James Brown" Como.

But there was also some shocking news on the music front: *Elvis got drafted.* Yes! They took the biggest rock star in the entire world, put him in the U.S. Army, and, as millions of teenage girls wailed in unison, shipped him off to Germany to defend us from the godless Communists. Can you imagine anything remotely like that happening today? Can you imagine the Army drafting, say, The Artist Formerly Known As Prince, sending him over to South Korea and putting him at the controls of a tank? I'm for it! Let's get at least *some* entertainment value for our defense dollars!

Speaking of the fight against Communism: In 1958 the Space Race got even more serious. Our side finally put a satellite, *Explorer I,* into space, but it was a pathetic weenie little device about the size of a lipstick tube. Also we had a lot of other launch attempts blow up before they got off the ground, so that the main tangible benefit of our space program was craters. Meanwhile the Russians were sending up large satellites, live dogs, entire working farm villages, etc.

On a prouder note, America continued to increase its lead over the rest of the world in the field of irritating TV commercials. Among the classics to appear in 1958 were:

- The Maypo breakfast-food commercial, which had millions of American children—we thought this was hilarious—constantly whining "I want my Maypo!" at our parents. About this same time there was a dramatic increase in tranquilizer usage among adults.

- The ad campaign for Mister Clean. It featured a really obnoxious jingle ("Mister Clean gets rid of dirt and grime and grease in just a minute!"), but the product sold really well, perhaps because Mister Clean was a muscular man in a very tight T-shirt who hung around the house, displaying a sincere interest in Mom's needs while Dad was off golfing his way up the ladder at Amalgamated Consolidated Conglomerated Coagulated. Sometimes Dad would come home and find Mom and Mister Clean smoking cigarettes, but he never suspected a thing.

This was also the year that saw the spectacular debut of one of the most dominant personalities in the history of TV advertising: Speedy Alka-Seltzer, who burst onto the scene like a comet and went on to win every major award in his field,[16] only to die tragically in 1983 from a drug overdose following the disclosure, by the *National Enquirer,* that he had no genitals.

1959

This was the year that Fidel Castro came to power. At first we thought he might be okay, but then he turned out to be a godless and bearded Communist, and so our Central Intelligence

---

16. His field was "tablet."

Agency established the Department of Overthrowing Fidel Castro, which now employs 17,000 people and in 1994 proudly celebrated its thirty-fifth consecutive year of service to a grateful nation.

Speaking of the nation, it got bigger in 1959 as Alaska and Hawaii were granted statehood. I personally viewed this as a bad thing, because in the fifth grade we had to memorize all the state capitals, and now there were two more of them, which did not make it any easier to catch up with the Russian fifth-graders, who as far as I knew didn't even *have* states.

In Cold War action, Vice President Dick visited Moscow and, during a tour of a model American home, got into what became known as the "Kitchen Debate" with Soviet Premier Khrushchev over the issue of what is the minimum number of ice cubes that you can leave in the tray without being morally obligated to refill it with water.[17] This issue would continue to divide the two superpowers until automatic ice-makers became standard, at which point the Soviet Union collapsed.

In consumer news, the American automotive industry, continuing its tradition of meeting basic consumer needs, came up with two major technological advances in 1959:

1. The Edsel.
2. Even bigger tailfins.

Despite these accomplishments, increasing numbers of ungrateful Americans were purchasing the cheap and reliable

---

17. According to the U.S. Supreme Court, ruling in the case of *Harold V. Hebblethwaite* v. *Mrs. Harold V. Hebblethwaite*, the minimum number is four.

Volkswagen Beetle, even though it had hardly any chrome and *no fins whatsoever.* At first the U.S. auto industry laughed at the VW, but finally it realized that, faced with this new low-end competition, it had to start making smaller, cheaper cars. But these would not be just any small cars; no, by God, these were going to be *really crappy* small cars, the theory being that consumers would be unhappy with them, and thus resume buying traditional American models that were designed more along the lines of freight locomotives.

And thus Detroit gave us the Ford Falcon, the Chevrolet Corvair, the Studebaker Lark, and the Plymouth Valiant (my mom's car). As the Germans, and then the Japanese, began to send over better and better economy models, Detroit shrewdly countered with a whole parade of stunningly bad cars, including the Ford Pinto, which exploded; the American Motors Gremlin, which appeared to have been designed by very young, poorly coordinated children; and of course the legendary Chevrolet Vega (I had one of these), a car that apparently had body rust installed on the assembly line. You know how, in old *Star Trek* episodes, when people get beamed up to the Enterprise, their bodies become sort of transparent, and then they disappear entirely? Well, the Vega would do that *while you were driving it.*

On a more positive consumer note, 1959 was the year that Mattel introduced the Barbie doll, which for generations to come would symbolize the ideal of American feminine beauty: an absurdly skinny woman with big gazombas. Also appearing for the first time was Choo Choo Charlie, who starred in many classic Good & Plenty commercials and was often seen at

Hollywood nightspots, partying until the wee hours with Speedy Alka Seltzer.

Speaking of celebrities, the big story of 1959, getting WAY more coverage than, for example, the Asian continent, was that Eddie Fisher got divorced from Debbie Reynolds so he could be married to Elizabeth Taylor for approximately twenty-five minutes. This was also the year that launched two classic movie genres:

- The "Gidget" genre, featuring various actresses portraying a typical teen gal of such transcendent perkiness that there was no possible way that narcotics were not involved; and
- The "Hercules" genre, featuring various beefy, heavily oiled actors playing a superhero who overcame the forces of evil and very stilted dialogue by singlehandedly picking up and breaking an impressive array of cheesy props.

When we weren't watching these movies, we were watching cowboys on TV. The broadcast schedule was totally dominated by westerns, including *Gunsmoke, Bonanza, Bat Masterson, Rawhide, Sugarfoot,* and *Irving A. Flubermayer, Prairie Proctologist.*

But for us young rock fans the big story of 1959 was the plane crash that killed Ritchie Valens, the Big Bopper, and my idol, Buddy Holly. This was the beginning of a pretty bad year for rock, which was being taken over by lame-o, soul-free "teen-idol" acts such as Pat Boone, Frankie Avalon, and, most pathetically, Fabian, whose vocal repertoire seemed to consist entirely of clearing his throat. The record industry seemed to think it could turn *anybody* into a rock star, the ultimate example being Edd Byrnes, an actor who played the character Kookie on the TV show *77 Sunset Strip*. Edd, who sang so badly he made Fabian sound like Ray Charles, recorded one of the worst songs in modern history—"Kookie, Kookie, Lend Me Your Comb"—which was filled with "hep" slang lingo that no actual young person of that era, or any other era, would ever actually use, such as: "I've got smog in my noggin, ever since you made the scene."

Rock was turning into a big-bucks industry. The music was getting slicker, more packaged, more nightclubby. We kids were hearing less of the raw, stomping sound that attracted us to rock in the first place. As the 1950s drew to a close, we felt a sense of expectancy, of waiting for some unknown thing to happen. But little did we know what was coming our way. Little did we suspect that rushing toward us, like a humongous hallucinogenic asteroid hurtling through space, was a decade that would radically change us; a decade that would see fundamental challenges to our most basic social and political institutions; and—above all—a decade during which we would spend a lot less time thinking about Buffalo Bob.

DISCUSSION QUESTIONS—THE FIFTIES

What was the name of the Cisco Kid's horse?
- a. Caramba
- b. El Horso del Cisco Kiddo
- c. Willy
- d. Alan Greenspan

Do you remember that little vent that cars used to have on the front windows, so on coolish days you could let a little fresh air in without causing a big draft? WHO THE HELL TOOK THAT LITTLE VENT AWAY?

The letters in "Adlai Stevenson" can be rearranged to spell "Saved Alien Snot." Explain.

Did the thought ever cross your mind that, when the rest of the family was out, Ozzie liked to dress up as Harriet? Cite specific examples.

How come Hugh Hefner, who spent most of his adult life surrounded by naked women, never seemed to be having any fun?

Guess how many Weinermobiles there are. Six!

Do you think the author will eventually grow tired of the Buffalo Bob joke? Why not?

4

The Sixties

Hell Yes, We Inhaled.

This was when the craziness happened.

Some of it was good craziness; a lot of it was bad craziness. It swirled all over the country, all over the world, like the colors on a tie-dyed shirt, wild and gaudy and often not making much sense. That era has a surreal quality now, as though it never really happened. (Certainly we tell our kids that a lot of it never happened.) But The Sixties did happen, with an energy and a vividness that have made all the decades that followed seem pretty bland. Not that bland is bad. Now that I'm 50, I definitely prefer bland. But God, The Sixties were *interesting*. Take, for example . . .

1960

This was truly a watershed year—the year that American society, having gone through the traumatic early Cold War era and developed into the mightiest military and industrial power on Earth, finally reached puberty and became interested in girls. Or at least that's what happened to me.

On a more global level, there was a huge stink when the Russians shot down an American U-2 spy plane. For a while the Eisenhower administration claimed that it was a weather plane that had strayed off course, but that story was blown when the Russians, pulling one of their most godless tricks, produced the actual pilot, whose name became a synonym for American Cold War blundering and failure: Buffalo Bob.

I'm sorry! I swear that is *really* the last time. The pilot was named Francis Gary Powers, and the Russians, after putting him on trial, sentenced him to ten years in jail. (Eighteen months later, he was returned to the United States via a trade in which the Russians got back their master spy, Col. Rudolf Abel, plus *two* first-round picks in the Secret Agent draft.)

The U-2 incident was a major embarrassment for the United States, and, as the nation geared up for the historic 1960 presidential race, there was a feeling of impending change in the air.[1] The Republicans basically had no choice but to nominate Dick Nixon, who received a somewhat reserved endorsement from President Eisenhower in the form of a brief written statement praising the vice president as "a protein-based life-form."

The Democrats, finally presented with a real shot at the White House, seriously considered going for the Trifecta and nominating Adlai Stevenson again (my parents had their

---

1. I personally did not notice this feeling, because, as I noted earlier, I had become interested in girls.

bumper stickers ready). But the nomination was won by John F. Kennedy, who became the ultimate symbol of coolness and glamor and teeth for many of us Baby Boomers, although I fear there will come a time when he is mainly remembered as being the father of John F. Kennedy Jr.

The 1960 race was the most exciting presidential campaign I ever saw. It was like a huge, months-long football game that everybody cared about—nothing like the campaigns we've been slogging through for the last couple of decades, which have stirred about the same level of public interest as the release of a new Slim Whitman album. Back in 1960, when we were always eyeball-to-eyeball with the Russians, the presidency was considered a hugely important job, unlike now, when the primary function of the federal government seems to be to produce repellent yet incomprehensible scandals, and politics is widely viewed as a joke, and the president is seen less as a national leader than as a celebrity—bigger than, say, Conan O'Brien, but nowhere near the level of Tom Cruise.

But in 1960 people took the presidency seriously. People were *involved* in that election. Just about every car had a Nixon or Kennedy bumper sticker, and you often heard people arguing about the candidates. What made it especially exciting is that it was such a close race. At first Kennedy appeared to have little chance, but the gap narrowed following the first-ever televised presidential debates, in which Kennedy appeared poised, while Nixon appeared nervous, especially when the tentacle came out of his mouth.

On election night, we stayed up late and watched the returns, and when I finally went to bed, the race was undecided. When I woke up the next morning, my parents were still in front of the TV, and the race was still undecided. I found out at school that Kennedy had won; a teacher told us this news, just as, three years later, a teacher would tell us that he had been shot.

But I'm getting ahead of myself on Defining Boomer Moments. The point is that, with the election of Kennedy, there was a shifting of the cultural gears—old to young; golf to touch football; bald to bushy-haired. (Now, of course, we're back to old and golf and bald.) And Kennedy was a Roman Catholic, which meant that, for the first time, we had a president who was not a white male Protestant. This raised the possibility that, one day in the not-so-distant future, we would have a president who was female or black or Jewish. Also we would travel to Europe for free on giant flying salamanders.

Speaking of prejudice: 1960 was the year that the civil rights sit-ins began in the South, which, despite the concerted efforts of me and my sister, was still extensively segregated. Of course the North was also extensively segregated, but the North was cooler about it. The South was blatant, and seemed to go out of its way to enforce its racial laws via violence-prone police officers with squinty eyes and stomachs the size of fully inflated life rafts. There was no question who the bad guys were, and as a result—this is my theory, anyway—it was easy for us young people who were attracted to the civil rights movement to start believing that we had the ability to instantly understand and solve complex social and political problems. This turned out to be good and bad: good, because it gave us confidence to fight some unpopular battles that needed to be fought; bad, because we tended to be a bunch of self-righteous assholes.

Along with the rise of social consciousness in 1960 came an increased interest in folk music. Large numbers of young people, including me, took guitar lessons and attempted to play songs such as "Michael, Row the Boat Ashore." The problem was that these songs contained a bunch of musical units called "chords." When the guitar teacher played chords, they sounded nice, but when we tried to play them—even after spending five minutes getting our fingers positioned properly on the strings—they made a dull, non-musical noise, THWUD, like an out-of-tune viola being struck with a dead raccoon. So our folk songs sounded like this:

Michael (five-minute pause) *THWUD the boat ashore,*
Al-le (five-minute pause) *THWUD ya . . .*

It could take us up to an hour to grind our way through a song. If we really had been on a rowboat with Michael, he'd have had no choice but to whack us with an oar.

On the pop music scene, 1960 was a significant year for several reasons:

- Elvis, having kept Western Europe out of godless Communist hands for his two required years, came home.
- Two of the most annoying songs in world history— "Running Bear" and "Itsy Bitsy Teenie Weenie Yellow Polka-dot Bikini"—were big hits.

- The musical genre known technically as "Songs About Teenagers Getting Killed in Cars, Which Would Make Us Sad Except for the Fact That These Songs Are So Smarmy" reached its peak with "Teen Angel" ("That fateful night, our car was stalled, upon the railroad tracks . . .")

But the biggest news on the pop scene was the dance sensation the Twist. This was huge. This might have been even bigger than the Hula Hoop. And you know why? Because it was a dance that *anybody* could do. *White people* could do it. People at wedding receptions everywhere still respond positively to the Twist for this reason.

In Armonk, there was a youth program called "canteen," wherein teenagers gathered on Friday nights at Harold C. Crittenden Junior High for basketball and dancing and minor vandalism. Generally we boys preferred basketball and vandalism; if we danced, it was only to slow songs such as "Put Your Head on My Shoulder." The fast songs were for the girls, who danced with each other.

But that changed with the Twist. We boys could do this dance; we practiced alone in our bedrooms. So on canteen night we could get out on the cafeteria floor in our tight white Levi's that ended about three inches above our shoes (*everybody* wore this look) and, with serious, purposeful expressions, we would swivel mechanically back and forth on the balls of our feet with all the relaxed spontaneity of motorized Christmas lawn ornaments. But we were fast-dancing! With girls! How cool was *that*?

Two notable movies came out in 1960:

- *Psycho,* which was notable because it resulted in a nationwide epidemic of b.o., caused by people not taking showers.
- *North to Alaska,* which was notable because it was the movie I went to on my very first date with an actual girl.

My date's name was Judy. I did not directly ask her on this date. I asked my friend Phil Grant, who was blessed with the fabulous and mysterious ability to talk directly to girls. Phil asked a girl named Nancy if she thought Judy would go on a date with me, and Nancy asked Judy, who said she would, and Nancy relayed this information to Phil, who told me.

The date was on a Saturday afternoon. I wore white Levi's. My mom drove. She was in the front seat, trying hard, like a good mom, not to exist; you could actually pass your hand through her. Judy and I sat in the backseat, three feet apart, saying absolutely nothing. I have no idea what happened in *North to Alaska,* because every brain cell I had was concentrated on the positioning of my left arm, which was resting on the hard back of Judy's seat, no more than one billionth of an inch from, but never coming into direct physical contact with, her shoulders. My arm stayed that way for the entire movie. I finally got all the feeling back in about 1982. But it was a fine date, and I told Phil so, and I just hope he passed the word along to Nancy, so that Judy found out.

1961

John Kennedy was sworn into office while a major snowstorm was going on in the Northeast, meaning that school was canceled in Armonk. So I went to the home of my friends Evan and Neil Thompson, and, sitting on the living-room floor in front of the TV, we watched the inauguration while playing Risk, a board game in which you build up your army and try to conquer your opponents' nations using the ultimate weapon: dice. I distinctly remember President Kennedy telling us that we should ask not what we could do for ourselves, but instead ask what we could do for our country. But I was only 13, and it was really cold outside, and I couldn't think of anything I could do for my country right at that moment, so I continued trying to take over the world.

This was also pretty much what the Russians were up to in 1961. For one thing, they started building the Berlin Wall, which led to one of those scary international displays of manhood that were always happening during the Cold War, with the Russians and us sending large masculine tanks to rumble around and see who had the longest guns. The Russians also were cozying up to Fidel Castro, thus forcing our top strategic brains to launch the Bay of Pigs invasion, a shrewd move that helped guarantee Castro would remain in power until his death, and possibly longer.

In the U.S., the rise in international tension helped to escalate Fallout Shelter Mania, with more and more Americans digging big holes in their backyards and installing concrete bunkers, which I would not be surprised to learn were manufactured by the Wham-O Corp. The thinking behind the fall-out shelters was that if there were a nuclear war you and your family would go underground and hang out for a few days, then, when it was safe, you'd come back up to the surface and rebuild society along with other foresighted shelter owners and radioactive cockroaches the size of mature sheep.

The Space Race also got more intense in 1961 when the Russians sent an actual godless person, Yuri Gagarin, into orbit. But we had been making progress on the non-exploding-rocket front, and finally we sent one of our own astronauts, Alan Shepard, on a suborbital flight. This was very exciting to us students at Harold C. Crittenden Junior High, in no small part because we got to get out of class to watch the launch on a TV in the auditorium. As I recall, there were many delays in the countdown, and the actual flight took less time than many Boomers today require to go to the bathroom. But at the time Americans were pretty darned proud: We had finally gotten on the space scoreboard, and on top of that, Roger Maris hit 61 home runs that year (no Russian hitter was even *close*).

Riding the wave of space mania, President Kennedy declared that, before the end of the decade, America would land a man on the Moon (he never said so, but I suspect that the specific man he had in mind was Richard Nixon). This was a very ambitious promise, but in The Sixties many people believed that the government was capable of great achievements, in contrast to the vastly lowered expectations of today, when the new programs proposed by presidents, amid much fanfare, are generally along the lines of a War on Dandruff.

On the cultural front, 1961 saw the appearance of two

books—the previously banned-in-America *Tropic of Cancer* by Henry Miller, and *The Carpetbaggers* by Harold Robbins—which introduced many males my age to an important literary theme: dirty parts. There may have also been plots in these books, but we never found out what they were; we were interested only in the sections—and we knew where these sections were—in which the authors used words such as "breast." A kid would get hold of one of these books and bring it to school, and we'd form a furtive clot around him in the hall, each of us experiencing the characteristically instantaneous, semipermanent boner of the adolescent male, as the kid read the breast parts aloud until a teacher approached, at which point we'd all scuttle off in different directions, holding our notebooks strategically in front of our pants.

Speaking of dirty parts: Among the hit records that year were "Will You Love Me Tomorrow," a song that we were pretty sure was about Going All The Way; and "Quarter to Three," a song that we were absolutely convinced contained dirty words, even though we could not agree what they were (this came to be known as the "Louie Louie Syndrome"); and "Blue Moon," a song whose explicit lyrics left nothing to the imagination. "Bomp ba-ba-bomp ba-bomp ba-bomp-bomp ba-ba-bomp ba-bom-bomp," stated these lyrics—adding, just in case you missed the point, "a-dang-a-dang-dang a-ding-a-dong ding, blue moon."[2]

Elsewhere on the 1961 cultural front, a young artist named Andy Warhol was inventing "Pop Art," which at the time was

---

2. *Source:* **Harvard University School of Syllables.**

dismissed by many people as nothing more than copies of soup-can labels, but which is now recognized as a brilliant innovation, although if you ask me, it's still basically copies of soup-can labels.

In fashion, some girls—the *tough* girls; the ones who hung out with the tough boys who styled their hair with what appeared to be transmission fluid—were wearing the "beehive" hairdo, which consisted of a huge mass of hair piled up on top of the head and held permanently in place by a volume of hairspray equivalent to the annual petrochemical output of Iran. There was a story that went around for years concerning a tough girl who hardly ever washed her beehive, and one day she started feeling some movement on her scalp, and she opened up her beehive and there was—*yuck*—a nest of spiders up there. Or, depending on who was telling the story, it was a nest of actual bees. This story probably wasn't true, but you heard it all the time in the Beehive Era. It was at least as plausible as the Domino Theory.

1962

This was the year when the big scare came in October, but it wasn't Halloween. The Russians put some of their godless missiles in Cuba, and when President Kennedy found out about it, he and Khrushchev got into a serious high-stakes international urination contest that became known as the Cuban Missile Crisis. Suddenly there were troops rumbling around in Florida and all the newspapers had giant scary headlines and the fallout-shelter contractors were working overtime and we were having air-raid drills every day at school, and even though we were at the age when a potential nuclear war is far less important than the discovery of a new zit, we could tell that our parents were really frightened, and we became frightened, too. Many people genuinely thought the world was about to blow up, and almost nobody knew what was really happening.

It's often said that the reason why we Baby Boomers became so rebellious and scornful of authority is that we were spoiled rotten and thus became obnoxiously self-centered. This is certainly true. But I think another reason, epitomized by the Cuban Missile Crisis, is that we grew up in a world where the highest authorities, on both sides of the Iron Curtain, regularly managed—with all their covert operations and their coups and their puppet governments and their spy planes and their atomic testing and their eyeball-to-eyeball confrontations—to get us into very scary situations, and then either told us nothing or lied to us. Eventually, we stopped trusting authorities. (Now, of course, we *are* the authorities, which is truly scary.)

Speaking of getting into situations: In 1962, the U.S. sent more combat troops to Vietnam, with the official explanation being that these were not combat troops. In the American South, the civil rights struggle was growing more confrontational and violent as many white people reacted with outrage to the idea that black people wanted—Who put this radical notion into their heads? Communists, probably!—to vote.

So 1962 was basically a pretty grim year. But there were some bright spots:

- The nation was treated to yet another wonderful Nixon Moment when Dick, having lost his bid to become governor of California, told the press, with typical grace and wit: "You won't have Dick Nixon to kick around anymore." Fortunately for humor columnists everywhere, this statement did not turn out to be true.

- The New York Mets started playing baseball (although not professionally).

- John Glenn became the first American astronaut to orbit the Earth, and the nation went crazy, and there was a monster ticker-tape parade in New York City, and Glenn was the biggest hero since Charles Lindbergh, and later he got into politics and was elected to the U.S. Senate, and he was there for a couple of decades, and now, as I write this, he's getting ready to go up *again,* which makes me wonder if I'll have to repeat ninth grade.

- A number of major new dances came out, including the Limbo, the Watusi, the Mashed Potato, and the Loco-Motion. Many of us Boomers can still perform these dances and regularly display our prowess at wedding receptions, bar mitzvahs, etc., even though this causes our children to sprint in embarrassment from the room.

- Marvel Comics introduced Spider-Man and the Hulk— a new, younger, hipper breed of superheroes who were more like our generation, as opposed to Superman and Batman, who were definitely grown-ups. We Boomers could relate to these superheroes. We could picture Spider-Man, on his day off, learning the Loco-Motion.

• In Liverpool, England, bandmates John Lennon, Paul McCartney, and George Harrison fired their old drummer, Pete Best, and replaced him with the final missing puzzle piece of what would some day be known as the Fab Four: Buffalo Bob.

1963

In the early part of the year, the big news story was the civil rights movement. Martin Luther King Jr. was leading demonstrations in Birmingham, Alabama, where the commissioner of public safety—a man named Eugene "Bull" Connor, who apparently got his public relations advice from the Wicked Witch of the West—decided to promote the public safety by attacking nonviolent demonstrators, in front of TV cameras, with dogs and fire hoses. The nation was appalled, and the civil rights movement, fueled by many idealistic young volunteers, surged ahead, and there were protest demonstrations all over the South that spring and summer.

In late August, 200,000 people gathered in Washington, D.C., for the historic march at which King gave his "I Have a Dream" speech. I was there. I rode down from New York City on a bus filled with other young people, mostly college students who'd worked that summer at a camp for city kids run by the New York City Mission Society, where my dad was executive director. The night before the big march, we attended a candlelight rally in Harlem; we held hands, black and white together, and sang "We Shall Overcome," and we were absolutely positive that we would. I got into a friendly argument with a bystander, a black man not much older than I, who laughed and assured me that nobody was going to overcome anything.

In some ways, I guess he was right, but the march on Washington was a euphoric and hopeful experience. We waved signs; we sang; we listened to speeches; we marveled at how many of us there were. We felt the thrill of doing something that was—back then—kind of daring (we were on a *protest march!*) and the sense of well-being that comes from believing that you are absolutely right and those who disagree with you are absolutely wrong. I can't imagine feeling that way about an issue today. And I don't know whether this is a good or a bad thing.

Another historic world-changing event occurring in 1963 was that New York State, disregarding the fact that I was a human hormone tornado with the emotional maturity of a bag of puppies, issued me a driver's license. The day it came in the mail, I took my mom's Plymouth Valiant station wagon and put maybe 125,000 miles on it. I believe that at one point I passed through New Zealand.

Is there a better feeling in the world than when you finally—after all those years of having your parents drive you everywhere, listening to their old-fart Patti Page music on the radio and sticking you in the backseat exchanging blows with your whiny little puke siblings—get the chance to drive a car yourself, all alone? Going wherever you want? Picking the radio station? Cranking up the volume? Steering with your right hand and resting your left hand casually on the car roof and keeping time with the music by tapping on the accelerator the way they told you never ever to do in driver education class?

No, there is not a better feeling. And what made it perfect for me was that 1963 was the height of the era of great car songs—songs whose very purpose was to be playing loud on the radio while you drove around with no purpose or destination. I'm talking about songs such as "Little Deuce Coupe," "Shut Down," and "409," songs that express a passion for cars in terms that are borderline sexual ("She's real fine, my 409 . . . My four-speed, dual-quad, Posi-Traction 409!").

Cars were hugely important to us. At Pleasantville High School, we went outside at lunchtime when the weather was good, and the guys who had their own cars would drive around the circle in front of the school, going maybe two miles per hour but revving their engines a lot to let the world know that they *could* be going 130 if not for the fact that they were being watched by Mr. Sabella, the assistant principal, a wide and formidable man who was capable of explaining school disciplinary policies by putting your head through a wall.

Across from the circle was The Corner, which was just off school property, which meant you could smoke and spit there. Dozens of guys would stand on The Corner, looking as cool as possible, and sometimes the revving cars would stop in front of the crowd, and their drivers would open their hoods, and everybody would gather around and examine their dual quads and spit in admiration. Guys would get into deep philosophical arguments about which was better, Ford or Chevy, these being the two major religions on The Corner.

In addition to car songs, there were these key musical developments in 1963:

- In England, the Rolling Stones were getting together, led by Keith Richards and Mick Jagger, who were then only in their mid-40s.
- As a few radio stations began playing records from another English group, we began to feel the first stirrings of the gentle breeze that would soon turn into Hurricane Beatles.
- Speaking of breezes: Bob Dylan recorded "Blowin' in the Wind," singing in a voice so unpolished, so non-showbizzy, so drastically unlike, for example, Bobby Vinton, that you either loved it or hated it, and the side you picked indicated pretty clearly whether you were going to be a willing participant in, or an opponent of, The Sixties.
- The Surfaris came out with the instrumental classic "Wipe Out," featuring three (count 'em!) chords and the drum solo that to this day touches the musical soul of all true Boomers, who sometimes play it with their hands on their office desks when their doors are closed and their co-workers think they're in there planning corporate strategy.
- Perhaps most important of all, the Kingsmen released their recording of the Richard Berry song "Louie Louie"—the song with the lyrics that nobody understood but everybody, including the Federal Bureau of

Investigation, was convinced were dirty; the song with the sledgehammer beat that makes everybody, including statues, want to get out on the dance floor and do the Alligator; the song that is musically so simple it can be learned in minutes by laboratory hamsters jumping up and down on guitars; the song that is responsible for the formation of God knows how many garage bands; the song that we should beam into space so that, if there are intelligent beings out there, they'll understand what Earth culture is truly all about, so they can avoid us; the song that I hope will be played at my funeral.

Also in 1963 the postal service introduced the ZIP code, which was a giant leap forward in the number-ization of America. Growing up, I didn't have many numbers in my personal life. There were no numbers in my address, which was "Elizabeth Place, Armonk, N.Y." So basically I had to remember my home phone number (ARmonk 3, 3119) and the number of the bus that took me home from school (Bus 7), and that was it for me, number-wise. Now, of course, in addition to my home and office phone numbers and addresses (with *nine-digit* ZIP codes), I have to remember my home fax number, my cell phone number, my wife's cell phone number, our home voice-mail retrieval number and secret code, our secret home alarm code, my secret password for logging on to the Internet, my secret ATM code, my secret telephone credit-card code, my office phone number, my office fax number, my office voice-mail retrieval number and secret code, the secret code for logging on to my office computer, and—this is the most important—the number of my office assistant, Judi Smith, because the fact that I have all these numbers and codes and passwords in my brain means there is little room for much else, so I often must call Judi to clarify certain details ("What's my name again?" "Is that my first name or my last name?").

On a more positive note, 1963 also saw the introduction of the Touch-Tone telephone. You young readers are probably not aware of this, but telephones used to have these rotary dials that you used to have to turn with your finger, which was hard work, plus you wasted precious seconds waiting for the rotary dial to mosey back to the start position after you dialed a digit (this could take *forever* if the telephone number had a lot of 9's or 0's in it). Also we had to walk 43 miles to school barefoot while churning our own butter, because there was a *Depression* going on, dammit, and in those days we . . . No, wait, sorry, I'm thinking of my parents' generation.

So on balance things were looking pretty good in 1963. Life was getting a little easier; there was happy and hopeful music in the air; in the South, the times finally seemed to be a-changin'. Not a bad year, really, until a warmish late November Friday when, many people have argued, The Sixties really started.

I found out from my Spanish teacher, Miss Nauman. She came into class late, and she started to say something, but she broke down. Finally she got it out: President Kennedy had been shot. A few minutes later another teacher came in and said they were saying on TV that the president was dead. Miss Nauman sat at her desk and sobbed. Some of the girls sobbed, too. We boys of course did not sob; in fact, on some incredibly self-centered adolescent level I think we were excited that something so dramatic was happening in our lives, plus we were obviously not going to be conjugating any Spanish verbs that afternoon. But we also felt uneasy; we were getting our first strong dose of the craziness, the sense of events whirling out of control, that was going to be with us, stronger and stronger, through the rest of The Sixties.

They let us out of school early, and the buses weren't there yet, so hundreds of kids went to The Corner to smoke and spit and talk about the assassination. A few guys, proving how cool they were, tried to joke about it, but most of us just stood there, not sure how to act. I remember wondering if the assassination would have any effect on the dance that was supposed to be held at the school the next night. I'd been looking forward to that dance.

Of course, the dance was canceled. Everything was canceled, and nobody did anything for the next few days except watch TV, which showed us the most amazing and shocking and desperately sad things. My mom wept for the entire weekend. When it was finally over, all of us who went through it had a set of shared memories and images permanently engraved in our brains. We also had a new president, Lyndon B. Johnson. We really wanted him to be a good man. A man we could trust.

1964

This was the year when the Beatles came over and stole rock 'n' roll away from the Fifties generation, away forever from Elvis. Girls were screaming in the streets; Ed Sullivan was wearing a mop-top wig; and it seemed as though every radio, even the ones that weren't turned on, was playing "I Want to Hold Your Hand."

The Beatles started the British Invasion—a massive influx of bands from England, including The Rolling Stones, The Dave Clark Five, The Who, Chad and Jeremy, Gerry and the Pacemakers, The Nigel Frompton Four, Peter and Gordon, Ted and the Catheters, Herman's Armpits, The What, The Stuart Montgomery Prendergast Whelk-Haberdasher IV Three, The When, Chad and Peter, The Cheesemongers, Gordon and Jeremy, The Where, Big Ben Johnson and the Noggin Men, The Whether, Jeremy and Jeremy, Scooter Weevil and The Twits, The Ear Tweakers, The How Much, and The Fronds. These bands produced a vast body of hit records, many of which, even now, more than thirty years later, still sound amazingly lame. Because the truth is that a lot of the British Invasion bands sucked.

But not the Beatles. If you were a 17-year-old suburban kid, which I was, they were the coolest thing you had ever seen. They wrote their own songs; they were smart; they were funny; they didn't take themselves seriously. I wanted desperately to be a Beatle. I would have worn my hair like theirs if not for the fear that Mr. Sabella would illustrate the Pleasantville High School hair policy by putting my head through a wall.

Speaking of policies: President Johnson got the historic Civil Rights Act of 1964 passed, but in the big cities a lot of people felt that equality wasn't coming fast enough. That summer, in New York and other cities, there were riots, as there would be in the summers to come.

Also that summer, Congress, responding quickly, decisively, and courageously to an incident that apparently did not happen, passed the Gulf of Tonkin resolution, which meant that President Johnson could do pretty much whatever he wanted in Vietnam. He assured the nation that he would "get us mired in a stupid unwinnable war."

No, sorry, that's what he actually *did*. What he assured the nation—with that somber facial expression of his, the one that was supposed to convey sincerity, but looked like heartburn—was that "we are not going to send American boys nine or ten thousand miles away from home to do what Asian boys ought to be doing for themselves."

That's right: Johnson, who was escalating the war as fast as he could, ran for president as the *peace candidate*. And what's more, most people believed him. I know my mom and dad did. People wanted to believe Johnson, because the Republicans had nominated Barry Goldwater, who decades later, after a distinguished political career, came to be widely perceived as a venerable statesman, but who in 1964 was widely perceived as a wacko fully capable of launching a nuclear strike against, say, Mexico. So the voters overwhelmingly elected somber, trustworthy Lyndon, who responded by sending more American boys off to do what Asian boys should have been doing for themselves.

Also in 1964, the Warren Commission released its report on the John F. Kennedy assassination. The commission concluded that Lee Harvey Oswald acted alone, and that settled *that*.

I am of course kidding. Within nanoseconds of the release of the Warren Commission report, a new American industry sprang up: the Paranoia Industry, which has grown over the decades to the point where it now employs three out of every ten Americans, and which has produced a massive body of solid evidence proving beyond a shadow of a doubt that Kennedy was in fact killed by a massive conspiracy whose members include—to name just a few—the FBI, the CIA, the military, big business, the Mafia, the Communists, the media, the Trilateral Commission, and the Presbyterian Church, as well as both Chad *and* Jeremy.

This is the same conspiracy that shoots down commercial aircraft, implants radio transmitters into people's skulls, and keeps large quantities of deceased alien beings stored in secret freezers for some reason, perhaps to use as hors d'oeuvres at the Conspiracy Member Christmas Party. This conspiracy is so widespread and powerful that it controls virtually every facet of American society, including the book publishing industry, which is why I am taking a great risk here when I reveal to you that, according to Top Secret documents I have obtained, within the next four months secret equipment will be installed on the nation's telecommunications system so that every person who answers a telephone will be bombarded by a new, high-frequency type of radiation that cannot be detected by the human ear, but that will cause an instant, irreversible, and horribly ███████████████████████████████████████
███████████████████████████████████████
███████████████████████████████████████
███████████████████████████████████████
███████████████████████████████████████
███████████████████████████████████████
███████████████████████████████████████

On the 1964 automotive front, Ford introduced the Mustang, which was immediately a big hit because it was cool and inexpensive and sporty. So naturally Ford turned the Mustang over to the technicians in the company's crack Division of Transforming Sporty Little Cars Into Big Ugly Bloated Turdmobiles. This is the same outfit that did such a good job on the Ford Thunderbird, which also started out as a sleek sports car and ended up being so large that U.S. Navy fighter planes could land safely on its hood.

On the 1964 nutritional front, Kellogg's introduced the Pop-Tart, the first toaster-based snack pastry designed for consumer use by humans. As an American, I am of course proud to live in the nation that developed this product, although I feel obligated to point out that an improperly prepared Pop-Tart can cause certain unpleasant side effects such as burning down your house. I found out about this several years ago when alert readers of my newspaper column began sending me newspaper articles from all over the country about house fires that were caused when toasters malfunctioned and failed to pop up their Pop-Tarts. I conducted a scientific experiment, using an inexpensive volunteer toaster from Kmart, and I found that if you hold the toaster lever down for about five minutes, a Kellogg's strawberry Pop-Tart will turn into the Snack Pastry Blowtorch from Hell, shooting flames a good twenty to thirty inches into the air. I wrote a column to publicize this danger, but the federal government chose to do nothing, and I still regularly receive news reports of Pop-Tart–related fires. I'm not saying that as a public health menace this problem is as serious as heart disease, but I would definitely rank it ahead of global warming.

In sports, a brash young boxer named Cassius Clay scored a stunning upset over Sonny Liston and became world heavy-weight champion. Clay then shocked the sports world by announcing that he had converted to the Black Muslim religion and henceforth would be known by the name that, in succeeding years, became one of the best-known and most respected in all of sports: Buffalo Bob.[3]

1965

This was the year I got my draft card. I was very happy about this, because the card served as legal proof that I was 18, which in those days meant that I could legally drink alcohol in New York State. It did not occur to me, at the time, that there was a downside to having a draft card.

When I turned 18 I was working as a counselor at a summer camp in Dutchess County, New York, called Camp Sharparoon (actual cheer segment: "Maroon! Maroon! Sharp-a-roon!"). To celebrate my birthday, my fellow counselors took me out to a local bar called The White Stag and bought me a drink called a "Singapore Sling," which was served to me in a large glass suitable for milkshakes. Thus I was able to go from having my first legal drink to barfing in the parking lot in roughly twenty minutes, which I believe is still the Dutchess County record.

Meanwhile, Lyndon Johnson was pushing through his Great Society legislation. (I don't mean to suggest that he was

---

3. I didn't put this joke here. The conspiracy put this joke here.

pushing it through at the exact moment when I was barfing in The White Stag parking lot. That was Lyndon's bowling night.) The Great Society was basically a plan to eliminate poverty, racism, hunger, ignorance, sloth, etc., by constructing enormous buildings in Washington, D.C., and filling them with tens of thousands of government employees with titles like Assistant Deputy Executive Administrative Liaison for Stapling. Years later, most of the Great Society programs were dismantled, and these employees wound up roaming the streets of Washington, offering to create bloated bureaucracies in exchange for food.

But back in 1965, there was hope in the air. Also, more and more, there was dope in the air. Most of us Boomers had been told, back in the 1950s, that marijuana was an extremely dangerous drug, like heroin, only more addictive.

"If you take just ONE PUFF of marijuana," our parents would tell us, in between drags on their king-size Chesterfields, "you'll be HOOKED FOR LIFE!"

By the summer of 1965, a lot of younger people were having serious doubts about these parental warnings, as they discovered from personal experience that marijuana did *not* cause you to become instantly addicted. Granted, it *did* cause you to become instantly stupid, not to mention capable of consuming, in just seconds, a wad of raw chocolate-chip cookie dough the size of a Yorkshire terrier. But at the time these did not seem like particularly bad effects, at least not when you compared them to, say, a Singapore Sling.

By 1965 more and more young people were also starting to ignore their parents' instructions on the topic of hair length.

It's hard to believe this today, but in The Sixties, hair length, especially on males, was a huge social issue, an issue that destroyed families and spawned much hatred and was the cause of God knows how many fights. In my late teens, I started to wear my hair longer—nothing extreme; pretty much the look favored by Moe of the Three Stooges—and when I was out in public, you'd have thought I was having unprotected sex with a llama right there on the sidewalk. People would laugh at me, or give me dirty looks and call me a hippie, or ask each other in a loud, self-amused voice—I can't tell you how many times I heard this hilarious question—"Is that a boy or a girl?" (Har! Good one!) Middle-aged guys in trucks would slow down next to me, roll down their windows, and scream, "FAGGOT!" These experiences contributed to my growing conviction that the vast majority of old people (defined as "people over 23") were morons.

That whole hair hassle seems *so* ridiculous today, now that succeeding generations have experimented with just about every conceivable hair mutation, and nobody is really shocked or offended by anything. Today, I sometimes see kids who are clearly trying to be outrageous, with fluorescent-colored, Mohawk-spiked hair, and giant spider tattoos, and nostrils, cheeks, lips, eyebrows, and tongues pierced by enough metal to fabricate a lawn tractor, and *nobody is paying any attention*. I feel sorry for these kids. I want to put my arm around them and cheer them up by saying: "If you'd been there in The Sixties, people would have beaten the *shit* out of you!"

Speaking of violence: Malcolm X was assassinated in 1965, and there were more riots—really bad riots, especially in L.A.—

that summer. The marches were still going on in the South, but the radiantly optimistic, we're-all-in-this-together spirit of the civil rights movement was fading fast. It was becoming less cool to hold hands and sing "We Shall Overcome"; it was becoming more cool to raise a fist and shout at people.

The United States was sending more and more troops to Vietnam; the draft boards were getting busier, and so were the antiwar protesters. Some young men even burned their draft cards, risking arrest, federal prosecution, imprisonment, and the threat of not getting served at The White Stag.

On the cultural front, 1965 was the year of the first TV commercial featuring Mister Whipple, the grocer who could not resist fondling Charmin-brand toilet paper. I'm not saying that this is the only reason why the nation went to hell for the next decade or so; I'm just saying it was a factor. On a more positive note, 1965 also saw the introduction of Gatorade and SpaghettiOs, two products that could survive a direct nuclear strike with no adverse effect on their taste, appearance, or nutritional quality.

On the musical front, the Beatles had a hit with "Yesterday," which was a troubling song for us young people because our parents actually *liked* it, which should have meant that we hated it, but we liked it, too. Fortunately for us this did not happen with many songs. It especially did not happen with the Rolling Stones' song "Satisfaction," which our parents thought was ugly and obscene, and which we therefore loved with a passion that made it the anthem of 1965, blaring virtually nonstop for months from the speaker of every teenager-operated car in America, with millions of teenaged fists pounding on millions of dashboards in unison to help Charlie Watts with the drums when Mick Jagger sang the part that went:

> *I can't GET NO! No no NO!*
> [Serious dashboard pounding here]
> *Hey hey HEY! That's what I say!*

There was another era-defining hit song that year: Bob Dylan's "Like a Rolling Stone," which was unlike any popular song before it—longer, looser, weirder, cooler . . . *hipper.* It was leading the way to the second half of The Sixties, which is when a huge mass of us Boomers left home and went to college. It would be a long, strange time before we came back.

1966

The bad news was that the riots continued and the war kept escalating. The national mood was ugly; the standard method of dialogue, on just about any issue, was to form mobs and shout.

The good news—at least for young men—was that it became fashionable for young women to wear miniskirts the size of gum wrappers. It was not possible for women wearing these skirts to bend over, or sit down, or even walk, without displaying their undergarments. It was dangerous for males to go outside, because they tended to develop a medical condition known as Miniskirt Rapture, wherein you'd be watching a woman walk in an extremely short skirt, and with every step a glimpse of underpants would come your way—*glimpse, glimpse, glimpse*—and your brain was so busy receiving this vital information that it stopped paying attention to anything else, and the next thing you know, you were being run over by a municipal bus, which happened to be on the sidewalk because the driver was also devoting his entire brain to receiving panty glimpses.

Speaking of brain malfunction: 1966 was the year when LSD became popular, especially on college campuses. At my school, the whole student body turned out to listen to a guest LSD lecturer, Richard Alpert, who had been fired from Harvard along with his associate, Timothy Leary, for advocating the use of psychedelic drugs. Alpert—who later became a mystic named Ram Dass, and still later became Richard Alpert again—told us, basically, that LSD was the coolest thing ever, and we should try some.

Naturally, being college students, we did not rush out and take a powerful, potentially harmful drug that we knew virtually nothing about just because some guy told us to. No sir. First we asked some hard questions, such as: "Where can we get some?" *Then* we rushed out and took it.

The claim was that LSD would "raise your consciousness," which made it sound as though it enabled you to perceive cosmic truths. That was not, in my experience, what actually happened, unless you define "perceive cosmic truths" as "see musical notes climb out of the speaker and dance around on the ceiling on skinny black legs." I never knew anybody who had a lasting philosophical insight under the influence of LSD. I knew a *lot* of people who became convinced that the walls were moving, but fortunately that particular insight usually wore off.

I think the best thing you can say about acid is that, if all went well, you had some very intense, era-defining experiences—some funny, some scary—that today you can laugh about with your fellow aging Baby Boomers and never discuss with your kids. The problem was that, if you were unlucky—as two people I know were—acid changed your brain in a bad way, and your brain never changed back. Old Ram Dass didn't mention that.

One positive aspect of the psychedelic movement is that the correct kind of hair to have was (don't ask me why) really *straight* hair, which is the kind I happen to have. This was the only era in my life when my natural hairstyle—hair coming out of the head and immediately heading toward the floor via the most direct route possible—was fashionable. During this era some of my wavy-haired male friends straightened their hair with powerful chemicals that are all probably banned by the government today. The straightening process took hours, and my friends' heads gave off toxic-waste aromas for days, and their hair came out all spiky, so they looked as though they were wearing hats made from dead porcupines. But they were cool!

Another cool psychedelic thing that everybody did was switch to eyeglasses with wire rims, which up to that time had been popular only with nuns. At about the same time, nuns started wearing plastic frames, so everything balanced out.

Speaking of nuns: In 1966 the Vatican decided that American Catholics could eat meat on Friday. This decision came too late for those of us, Catholic and non-Catholic alike, who had spent many a Friday lunch period in our school cafeterias staring glumly down at meatless entrees such as the dreaded "tuna casserole," which school cafeterias manufactured by the ton, using government-surplus ingredients that had been rejected by the military on the basis of being too dense.

In another major 1966 food development, the Pillsbury Doughboy was created. Don't even *try* to tell me that drugs were not involved.

On the cultural scene, 1966 brought one of the great fad TV shows, *Batman,* which went out of its way to be awful, and thus was hugely popular. We college students never missed an episode of *Batman,* assigning it the highest priority in our busy schedules, even higher than hair straightening. We were also very conscientious about watching three other new shows—*The Avengers, Mission: Impossible,* and of course *Star Trek,* the now-classic series in which a cast of courageous individuals, wearing what appear to be pajamas, explores the universe and discovers that it is positively teeming with hostile extraterrestrial beings, many of which speak English with Russian accents.

There were many fine hit songs in 1966, but none as wondrous as the Troggs' "Wild Thing," which has to rank up there with "Louie Louie" on the all-time list of three-chord garage-band rock songs so fundamentally mindless that they can be performed successfully no matter how untalented or otherwise impaired the band members are. I know! I've been there! Many times in the late Sixties, while a member of a really mediocre band called "The Guides,"[4] I peered out through my

---

4. Later, we became "The Federal Duck." And then we became "Ram Dass."

wire-rimmed glasses at a stomping, gyrating, seriously buzzed crowd of college students and together we all shouted, with real emotion, the words:

> *WILD THING! You make my HEART SING!*
> *You make EVERYTHING GROOVY*

You can call me a misty-eyed idealist if you want, but in those moments, I believed that, in some crazy way, I really *was* a Trogg.

1967

This was the year of the semi-mythical Summer of Love, although there were also large quantities of hate going around—more inner-city riots, more war, more protests, more guys in pickup trucks yelling at guys like me about our hair, and more guys like me flipping the bird back. But there *was* a lot of love, at least according to the 1967 hippie definition of "love," which was: "a feeling of random mellowness and generalized goodwill, usually caused by chemicals."

This was the year of Flower Power, and meditation, and the Maharishi Mahesh Yogi, and Ravi Shankar playing sitar music, which many of us actually did not care for, but which we tried hard to like because the Beatles liked it, and they had become gods. And the message from the gods was: *I get high with a little help from my friends.* They conveyed this message via the ultimate symbol of 1967, and really of all of the Sixties: *Sgt. Pepper's*

Lonely Hearts Club Band. Today, *Sgt. Pepper's* seems almost quaint, but in 1967 it seemed impossibly cool—a mysterious musical acid trip, so different from the here's-a-song, here's-another-song format of the albums that had gone before it. For much of the year, *Sgt. Pepper's* seemed to be coming out of every speaker in every college dorm room, over and over, wearing a deep, permanent groove into our brains.

. . . with a little help from my friends . . .

This was also the year when the rumor went around that if you dried some banana skins in an oven, then scraped the gunk off the inside of the skins and smoked it, *you would get high!* This rumor was so stupid that we of course believed it. We bought bananas by the dozens, and we smoked the gunk, and many of us convinced ourselves that we were getting high, although it was really just hyperventilation, because you had to puff like a freight locomotive to keep the gunk lit. We would have gotten just as high smoking peat moss.[5]

This was also the year when I paid $2 to get into a rock concert of local bands in Washington, D.C., where I was working as a summer intern. The concert was in an auditorium with all the seats removed, so we sat on the floor, which had been painted with Day-Glo paint. After the local bands played, the organizers announced that there would be a special guest artist, and they set up this gigantic amplifier, the biggest one I

---

5. **Important note to impressionable young people: Do NOT smoke peat moss! One puff, and you will be HOOKED FOR LIFE!**

had ever seen, in the middle of the stage, and out walked: Jimi Hendrix. Whom none of us had ever heard of. He was wearing a bright orange suit, and his hair looked like an approaching thunderstorm. He cranked the amp volume up to about a million, picked up his guitar, and

WHOMMMM

we were literally blown over, onto our backs, by the sound. Today, as a person in his fifties, I would hate to be subjected to that level of noise. But then, in the Summer of Love, with love coursing through my bloodstream, it was a religious experience.

Another positive musical development of 1967 was the introduction of the audiocassette tape, which was very important because it replaced the dreaded eight-track cartridge. Remember the eight-track, aging boomers? Sure you do. That was the mutant technology that we all installed in our cars so that we could listen to our favorite songs, except that, the way the eight-track was designed, you could never seem to *find* your favorite song. For every minute you spent listening to actual music, you spent what seemed like a half hour randomly pressing the fast-forward button or the change-track button, getting more and more involved in this task until finally you were devoting 97 percent of your attention to the task of finding the song and 3 percent to steering. There probably would have been a lot of accidents, if not for the fact that you tended to be driving very, very slowly. You'd think that you were barreling right along, at the very limit of your ability to react, and you'd look at your speedometer, and it would say: 9 miles per hour. Which was okay; you were in no hurry. In fact, you could no longer remember where you were going.

That was 1967: driving really slow, trying to find a song on the eight-track. Feeling love.

1968

If you want a strong example of how much difference a decade can make, cast your mind back to 1958, when the mass youth activity sweeping the nation involved Hula Hoops and the big military-draft controversy involved Elvis.

Things had definitely changed by 1968. In fact, things pretty much sucked. For starters, Martin Luther King Jr. was assassinated, and that snuffed out the waning, sputtering goodwill spirit of the civil rights movement.

I learned of the King assassination while walking across the Haverford College campus. The guy who told me about it was one of our campus radicals; almost every campus had some, by 1968. These were guys (most of them were guys, anyway) who thought that capitalism was a terrible idea and all cops were "pigs" and Chairman Mao was a swell person. The campus radicals believed they spoke for, and thought for, The People. They were *always* talking about what The People wanted, and what The People needed, although it seemed as though the only actual people that the campus radicals spent any time with were other campus radicals. They had spent several whole semesters thinking about what was wrong with America, and they had concluded that the only solution to our problems was for The People to rise up in violent revolt against The System, after which we would set up a new, better society, according to the wise principles laid down by campus radicals.

So anyway, this campus radical came up to me, very excited, and said: "Did you hear?"

"Hear what?" I asked.

"Martin Luther King was assassinated!" he said. He was smiling. He was *happy* about this.

"It's gonna happen now!" he said. "The blacks are *really* gonna riot now!"

This is when it began to dawn on me that there was a serious competition going on in America to see who could be the biggest group of assholes: the right-wing assholes who thought that the Vietnam War was a good thing, as long as they personally did not have to go over to Vietnam and get shot at; or the left-wing assholes who thought that what we really needed was for more people to shoot each other here at home.

It seemed as if both sets of assholes were winning in 1968. The King assassination did, in fact, result in terrible riots; and the Vietnam War, despite its growing unpopularity, became the longest in American history, with more U.S. troops over there than ever, and more men being drafted, and no end in sight.

The 1968 presidential campaign did not give cause for hope. It was a bizarre series of events, starting when Eugene McCarthy, running for the Democratic nomination as an antiwar candidate, did surprisingly well in New Hampshire. Then

Lyndon Johnson, realizing that he had blown his presidency, shocked the world by announcing that he would not seek reelection. Then Bobby Kennedy got into the race and looked as though he had a chance to win the nomination, until— somehow, that godawful year, you *knew* this was coming—he was gunned down. By then the whole political process was lurching out of control, so that when the Democrats tried to hold their convention in Chicago, it wasn't a convention at all: It was a screaming, tear-gas-and-billy-club hatefest. Out of this mess came the Democratic nominee, poor old Hubert Humphrey, who seemed like a nice guy, but who was tainted by the fact that he was Johnson's vice president. Plus, his name was "Hubert." Plus, 1968 was no year for nice guys.

And so, after all that turmoil, the voters ended up electing, by the barest of margins, their new president and leader, a man whose career had seemed to be over; a man who many people thought had permanently disappeared from the national scene. That man, of course, was: Buffalo Bob.

No, it was Richard M. Nixon, who won, in part, because he claimed that he had a plan to end the war, which he would reveal after he was inaugurated. A Secret Plan! You could always count on Dick to keep the surprises coming. Another one was his selection for vice president. This turned out to be Spiro Agnew, the relatively unknown governor of Maryland, who resembled a large, Brylcreem-smeared attack weasel. Spiro would go on to distinguish himself by (1) harshly criticizing war protesters and the media; (2) staunchly advocating "law and order"; and (3) accepting cash bribes in office.

This, then, was how we ended 1968: A president leaving

office in failure; two leaders shot dead; an angry, divided, increasingly violent nation mired in an unpopular war; and the reins of power being handed over to . . . Dick and Spiro.

This is not to say that there were no bright spots at all in 1968. In fact, there were several:

- McDonald's introduced the Big Mac, an advanced cholesterol-delivery system based on a complex formula that was years ahead of anything being developed by Soviet hamburger scientists.
- Some excellent new TV shows, including *Hawaii Five-O*, in which Jack Lord personally apprehended every criminal on Oahu; and *Rowan & Martin's Laugh-In*, in which a cast of wacky comics kept Americans in stitches week after week after week by endlessly repeating the hilarious phrase "Sock it to me!" Okay, you had to be there.
- In another exciting TV development, the authorities decided to permit advertising that explicitly discussed intimate personal problems. This cleared the way for those commercials that always seem to come on when you're eating dinner, wherein actors pretending to be normal humans go into the drugstore and talk loudly with the pharmacist about problems that most people will not even mention to their own selves:

PHARMACIST: What's wrong, Mr. Johnson?
MR. JOHNSON: It's these darned hemorrhoids! I feel like I'm sitting on a burning grapefruit!
PHARMACIST: Try this product! It's new AND improved!

MR. JOHNSON: Great! I'll smear some on my butt right here in the drugstore!
MRS. JOHNSON: Will that product also eliminate the unpleasant aroma in my feminine region?
PHARMACIST: It certainly will, according to clinical studies!
MRS. JOHNSON: Good! Because I am giving off a stench that would fell a bison!
MR. JOHNSON: You're telling me!
(They all laugh heartily)

We take these commercials for granted today, but in 1968 they were a brand-new concept. Also entering the American consciousness that year were the songs "Honey" and "MacArthur Park." Maybe we should have just skipped from 1967 to 1969.

1969

Come to think of it, maybe we should have skipped 1969, too. This was the year that Nixon was inaugurated, and it soon became clear that his Secret Plan to end the war consisted, basically, of continuing the war. This led to new, massive anti-war protests, and to heightened opposition to the draft.

I, personally, was very concerned about the draft: This was the year I graduated from college, and my draft board was expressing a keen interest in my future plans. I did not want to go to Vietnam. Partly this was because I thought the war was wrong and stupid. Partly this was because I didn't want to get killed. I spent much of my senior year wondering what to do. A lot of guys were in that situation. Some joined the National Guard; some went to Canada; some went to jail. A lot of guys tried for medical or psychological deferments, which were becoming harder and harder to get.

Guys tried all kinds of strategies, things like eating huge quantities of egg whites, which I think was supposed to do something to your blood. I know a guy who shot off his trigger finger. I know another guy who went to the bathroom in his underpants for several days, then wore them to his draft physical, on the theory that he would smell so disgusting that the doctors would reject him solely so that they wouldn't have to get any closer to him (this strategy worked).

I applied to be classified as a conscientious objector, or C.O., which meant that I would be excused from serving in the army on the basis of being morally opposed to all violence. That was not really my belief; although I *was* morally opposed to the Vietnam War, I'm pretty sure I would have been willing to fight in, for example, World War II. The C.O. status was not supposed to be granted to people who selectively opposed specific wars, like me. But I didn't know what else to do.

On a July evening, about a month after I finished college, I was called in for a hearing before my local draft board, in Peekskill, New York. There were about a dozen of us seeking C.O. classification; one by one we were called into a room with the draft-board members, who were mostly blue-collar workers, mostly veterans, with a reputation for being hostile to C.O. applicants. But they were easy on me, and seemed sympathetic to my application. I think this was for two reasons: my dad was a Presbyterian minister, and my college, Haverford, had a strong Quaker tradition. The draft board approved my C.O. classification. I compared notes with the other applicants, some of whom, I thought, were far more deserving of C.O. classification than I was. They all said that the board members' questions to them had been hostile. I'm pretty sure I'm the only one of us who got approved. When we left that night, some of the other guys were talking about Canada.

As a C.O., I was required to perform two years of what was called "alternative service," doing some job that my draft board deemed to be in the national interest. My board decided that I would do my two years as—don't ask me to explain this—a bookkeeper for the national headquarters of the Episcopal Church, in New York City. That's what I did during the war: accounts payable. I never got close to combat, unless you count the IRT subway at rush hour.

Like many guys who managed to stay out of Vietnam, I've spent a lot of time over the years thinking about what I did, and feeling guilty about the fact that other guys, including guys I knew, went over there, and some of them died over there. But I feel far more sorrow than guilt. To me, most of the guilt belongs to the people who got us into the war without knowing what they were doing, and the ones who lied about what was happening, and the ones who kept sending draftees over there long after it had become clear that it was a terrible mistake. That's what made the late Sixties and early Seventies so surreal, if you were a draft-age male: The nation was clearly sick of the war; the previous president had been ousted because of it; the current president had been elected largely because he said he would get us out of it; the soldiers who were coming back from Vietnam were saying, overwhelmingly, that it was a tragic joke; and *still* our government was sending more young men over there to die.

So I'm not scornful of the guy who pooped in his underpants. As far as I'm concerned, he was behaving more honorably than, say, Henry Kissinger.

There was one great moment of national unity in 1969: The night of July 20, when we all tuned in to watch astronauts Neil Armstrong and Buzz Aldrin walking around *on the freaking Moon.* It was an amazing thing to see; nearly 94 percent of the nation's households were watching on TV. This raises the question: What were the other 6 percent watching? *Hee Haw?*

The only bad thing about the Moon landing is that for the next twenty years, hardly a day would go by without some politician or op-ed columnist asking some whiny question like: "If we can land a man on the Moon, how come we can't develop a workable program for identifying the warning signs of gum disease among lower-income children in grades three through eight?" Fortunately we no longer hear that type of question, because we're quite confident, as a nation, that we no longer *can* land a man—excuse me, a person—on the Moon. It's a real load off our minds.

Speaking of amazing accomplishments: In 1969, the New York Mets, who for most of their brief existence had played professional baseball about as well as the Washington Monument floats, won the World Series. The day they clinched it, I was at the Episcopal Church headquarters in midtown Manhattan, working on my accounts payable, and I walked out of my building to see a big circle of office workers holding hands and dancing the hora smack in the middle of Second Avenue as streams of computer printouts swirled down from office windows above. It was the happiest group of people I've ever seen in New York, even happier than the crowd I once saw that gathered to cheer for an elderly pedestrian who was standing in the middle of an intersection, stopping all traffic, using his cane to slowly but relentlessly beat on the hood of a honking taxi.

In other 1969 news, Teddy Kennedy, heir to the Kennedy mystique, drove his future off a bridge. Dwight Eisenhower, ultimate symbol of the placid Fifties, died. Paul McCartney did not die, but quite a few people, having carefully studied clues on various Beatles albums, concluded that he had. Paul insisted repeatedly that he was still alive, but these people refused to believe him. They had clues!

Speaking of drugs: 1969 was also the year of Woodstock, the high-water mark of the hippie era, a historic cultural gathering of 500,000 young people and two portable toilets. For three days, people got high, got naked, got muddy, got to listen to all the big musical acts—Hendrix, Crosby, Stills & Nash, The Jefferson Airplane, The Who, The Grateful Dead, Perry Como.

I missed the whole thing. I had to work. But for my 50th birthday, a friend of mine gave me a computer CD-ROM version of Woodstock. "It's an even better trip on CD-ROM!" states the box. Unfortunately, what with one thing and another, I've never gotten around to playing the CD-ROM. I'll probably regret this thirty years from now, when I'm in a home for the elderly, and all the other elderly are sitting around in their wheelchairs, saying: "Remember the Wood-stock CD-ROM? That was *awesome,* dude!"

DISCUSSION QUESTIONS—THE SIXTIES

How come we never have any new dance sensations like the Twist anymore? Or do we still have them but our kids just don't tell us about them?

Do cars still have "quads"? What are "quads"?

What was the name of the Indian maiden with whom Running Bear was in love?
   a. Little White Dove
   b. Running Snake
   c. Little White Snake
   d. Alan Greenspan

Boy, postal service sure has improved since we got the ZIP code, huh?

Do you remember those little stickers that Democrats put over urinals during the 1964 campaign that said, "Deposit Your Goldwater Here"? Well, I do.

You think I'm kidding about the Pop-Tart danger, right? If only.

Do you remember the episode of The Avengers *wherein the villain invents a super-deadly cold virus that kills you with one sneeze, and Steed ends up fighting the villain inside a gigantic model of a nose, so you can't see who's winning, and you hear a sneeze, and the villain drops out of one of the nostrils, like a gigantic booger? Now* that *was a climax.*

Whatever happened to the Troggs?

Did you inhale? Explain.

5
The Early Seventies

Maturity Rears Its Ugly Head.

W hen the Seventies started, Sixties Fever was still raging; it would continue to rage for the early years of the new decade. Finally it broke, and the country started to settle down. So did many Boomers, as they began to run head-on into some important Truths of Life, such as:

- You may have gone to college and learned how to solve all of society's problems, but when you get out in the real world, nobody ever asks you to how to solve all of society's problems. In the real world, what people ask you are questions like: "Can you make coffee?" and "Where's the rent money?"
- It sounds like a terrific idea to live on a commune, raise your own organic vegetables, share all your possessions with your friends, and practice "free love"—until you

discover that "organic" is a scientific term for "extensively chewed by insects," and that your friends don't necessarily have possessions that you want to share, but some of them do have lice.

• If you keep doing drugs, at some point you cease being a bold explorer of the human consciousness and start being a person who sits around drooling.

• No matter how hard you try to like sitar music, it sucks.

And so, gradually but inevitably, most Boomers started to change, becoming less and less like Che Guevera, more and more like Pat Boone. They were growing up. But not right away. First everybody had to get through . . .

1970

The Nixon administration, continuing to carry out its Secret Plan to end the war and bring the troops home, invaded Cambodia. This led to more protests, especially on college campuses, including Kent State, where National Guardsmen opened fire and four people were killed. This led to many more campus protests, and the rhetoric on both sides got more vicious than ever.

It seemed as though everybody in America was angry. The day after Kent State, I got on the elevator at work, and another staff worker, the executive secretary to a high-ranking church official, got on there with me, and I, assuming that she would agree, said: "Isn't that awful about Kent State?" And she snapped at me: "They wouldn't have gotten shot if they hadn't been there." And I snapped back: "They *belonged* there! It's a *college!*" And the door opened, and she got off the elevator, and that was the last time we ever spoke.

The antiwar protests led to pro-war—or, more accurately, anti-antiwar—protests, including a big one in Manhattan in which thousands of people, many of them construction workers, marched through the streets. I went out and watched that one during my lunch hour. My main memory is of two men, both about my age: One was a crew-cut protester, wearing a tool belt; the other was a long-haired guy on the sidewalk. The long-haired guy started yelling "STOP THE WAR! STOP THE WAR!" The crew-cut guy ran over to him and, stopping just short of making physical contact, began yelling "BETTER DEAD THAN RED! BETTER DEAD THAN RED!" The two of them stood there, close enough to exchange spittle, screaming slogans at each other. That was political discourse in 1970.

American society wasn't the only thing coming apart: This was also the year that the Beatles—perhaps because of internal jealousy over the attention Paul was getting for being dead—broke up, and nobody has come close to replacing them. Speaking of dead: Jimi Hendrix, proving the truth of the old maxim "Never try to put all the chemicals in the entire world into your body at the same time," went to The Big Gig in the Sky that year. So did Janis Joplin, although I keep hoping she'll come back from the grave to strangle whatever advertising slimeball came up with the idea of using her voice to make a Mercedes-Benz commercial.

I know I'm going to sound like the classic old stuck-in-The-Sixties fart when I say this, but: I think 1970 was the year that rock music began a decline from which it has not recovered. We lost Janis, Jimi, and the Beatles; we got Bread, The Carpenters, and The Partridge Family. We were entering the Era of Weenie Music. Lurking ominously just over the horizon was: Disco.

On the other side of the coin, 1970 did bring many positive cultural developments. Okay, maybe "many" is not the best word. Maybe a better word would be "two." One was *The Mary Tyler Moore Show*. All of you males out there who spent the early Seventies sincerely in love with Mary Tyler Moore, raise your hand now. I thought so.

The other important cultural development was also a TV show, and one that would become a symbol of America every bit as significant as the Empire State Building, the Grand Canyon, and the Pez Dispenser: *Monday Night Football*. There have been many changes in the cast, which over the years has included such legendary names as Howard Cosell, Don Meredith, Frank Gifford, Keith Jackson, Reggie Jackson, the Jackson 5, Walter Cronkite, and Buffalo Bob. But one thing has not changed: Year in and year out, regardless of which teams were playing, *Monday Night Football* has delivered the most consistent and prolific output of football clichés the sports world has ever seen, as shown by this chart:[1]

---

1. *Source:* The Library of Congress.

MONDAY NIGHT FOOTBALL CLICHÉS (1970–1998)	
Number of Times Used	**Wording**
72 MILLION (EST.)	"THIS IS A CRUCIAL THIRD-DOWN SITUATION."
887,342	"THERE'S SOME REAL HITTING GOING ON OUT THERE."
512,003	"THAT WAS A COSTLY FUMBLE."
412,002	"THAT WAS A COSTLY PENALTY."
312,001	"THAT WAS A COSTLY INTERCEPTION."
201,092	"IF YOU SAY 'COSTLY' OVER AND OVER, IT SOUNDS REALLY WEIRD: 'COSTLY COSTLY COSTLY.'"
143,112	"THAT'S A PLAY HE HAS JUST GOT TO MAKE."
81,245	"HE HAS JUST GOT TO MAKE THAT PLAY."
51,417	"THERE IS NO KIND OF ROOM FOR THAT KIND OF PLAY IN THIS KIND OF GAME."
43,454	"HE MAY HAVE TORN HIS ANTERIOR CRUCIATE LIGAMENT, BUT WE WON'T SPECULATE."
6,921	"I FORGET WHICH TWO TEAMS ARE PLAYING IN THIS PARTICULAR GAME."
341	"HEY, WE CAN SAY ANYTHING WE WANT, BECAUSE OUR VIEWERS HAVE BEEN ASLEEP FOR OVER AN HOUR!"
78	"FRANK, WHAT ARE YOU USING ON YOUR HAIR? THE HIGH-LIGHTS LOOK SO NATURAL!"
56	"SOME OF THESE PLAYERS HAVE *TERRIFIC* BUTTS!"

1971

The weirdest thing happened in 1971: President Nixon, after twenty-five years of loudly condemning China and denouncing anybody who was suspected of being friendly toward the Chinese, suddenly decided that, hey, China was okay after all!

Historians are still not sure what caused this radical change of heart in Dick. Maybe he ate a really tasty dish of Kung Pao chicken; maybe he got a signal from his planet of origin. All we know for sure is that one minute we were archenemies of the godless Chinese Communists, and the next minute our national Ping-Pong team was over there drinking toasts with their national Ping-Pong team.

What made this especially confusing was that we continued to officially hate the godless Russian Communists. And of course we also still hated the godless Vietnamese Communists, so, in accordance with the Secret Peace Plan, we continued to wage war against them. The antiwar movement continued to grow, especially after the *New York Times* started publishing the Pentagon Papers, a secret government study concluding that the government had consistently lied to the public about Vietnam. The Nixon administration responded by taking legal action[2] against the people who had made the papers public, on the theory that it is very bad, in a democracy, for the public to find out what the government is doing. To prevent this kind of thing from happening again, the administration set up a special unit to stop leaks, which became known as "The Plumbers." Also formed that year was the Committee to Reelect the President, which became known, wonderfully, as CREEP. Both of these operations seemed, at the time, to be staffed by very serious men in suits; nobody suspected that they would wind up providing the nation with some of the wackiest moments in the history of federal comedy.

---

2. And illegal action, we later found out.

But the main distinguishing characteristic of 1971 is that it was the Year of Alarming Trends. One of the worst—we have still not recovered from it—was the "smile" button. This was a little yellow button that looked like this: ☺. The idea was that you pinned it on your lapel, thus conveying the heartfelt message: "I have no nose." In 1971, the smile button suddenly started appearing everywhere; probably the Russians were behind it. Pretty soon people were drawing little smiley faces in every kind of written communication:

> # ...AND IF WE DO NOT GET **ALL** OF THE RANSOM MONEY BY 5 P.M. SHARP, YOU WILL NEVER SEE YOUR BABY AGAIN
>
>

Today the smiley face continues to spread like tropical gonorrhea via the Internet, where many people find it virtually impossible to end a sentence without a little sideways smiley face :-) —which is eventually going to replace the period as the standard sentence-ending punctuation mark. Thus future generations will have to come up with an even cuter and more inane symbol to indicate what a swell mood they are in when they end their sentences:

Dear Mr. Jones: Your test results indicate that you have cancer.

Some other alarming trends that got rolling in 1971 were:

- **est Seminars.** These were seminars wherein you paid money to learn the secret of happiness, which is . . . Well, unfortunately I can't tell you the secret of happiness. It's a secret. You have to take the est seminar to get it. I can tell you, however, that this was the beginning of the California-spawned desperate-for-fulfillment New Age rent-a-guru movement, in which people seeking to have meaning in their lives decided that they could obtain it by paying money to sit in a hotel room for several days and scream and cry and not be permitted to go to the bathroom and be yelled at by the seminar leader. Things ultimately got so bad in the fulfillment movement that people were paying money to listen to lectures by actress Shirley MacLaine, who has actual, visible bats flying in and out of her ears. Fortunately, today more and more people are coming to their senses and finding fulfillment by returning to traditional values or, in my case, beer.
- **Waterbeds.** The waterbed trend was similar to the fulfillment movement, in the sense that you paid for something that was supposed to bring you happiness, but you wound up with something less fulfilling, in this case motion sickness and floor damage.
- **Frank Sinatra Retiring.** Frank's first official retirement was in 1971; it went so well that he started retiring on pretty much a full-time basis, and ultimately wound up spending more time retiring than many singers spent having their actual careers.

- **David Cassidy AND Donny Osmond.** They both had hit records in 1971. Meanwhile, Duane Allman died. How is *that* fair?

- **Ten-Speed Bicycles.** Before 1971, American bicycles had only one speed.[3] They also had big fat American tires and large, comfortable American seats ideally suited for the big, fat American butt. You rode these bicycles sitting up, the way God intended.[4] But in 1971 it became trendy to ride European-style skinny-tired ten-speed racing-style bicycles, the kind where you have to ride all hunched over, constantly having to change speeds while your butt is being savagely assaulted by a seat the same size as, and made from the same material as, a hockey puck. People defend these bicycles by saying that they are efficient. I say: *So were the Nazis.*

- **Night World Series Games.** In my youth, World Series games were played during the day, and *everybody* followed them closely, so that during the games, the nation's productivity dropped to zero. If the godless Russians had really been smart, they would have invaded the United States during a World Series game. Nobody would have noticed them. They could have walked right into the White House, because all the guards would have been huddled around a transistor radio, eyes riveted to the little speaker, waiting for it to

---

3. Slow.
4. See the Bible, Book of Herb, chapter 4, verse 12: *And God saideth unto Hezekiah, he saideth, "You should rideth a bicycle sitting up."*

tell them what happened on the 3–2 pitch. In 1971, the executives in charge of television and baseball, seeing this pure and passionate love affair between Americans and the World Series, said: "Hey! We need to ruin this!" And so they came up with the concept of televising World Series games at night, starting late enough so that all of the East Coast viewers would be asleep by the end of the National Anthem. They also started scheduling the games later and later in the year, which meant that the World Series became less of a Fall Classic and more of a Winter Olympics event, as epitomized by Game 5 of the 1997 World Series, when two Cleveland Indians outfielders became lost in snowdrifts and were eaten by wolves.

• **"Socially Relevant" TV Commercials.** Before 1971, TV commercials generally tried to sell you products by conveying some message that was at least vaguely related to the actual product. For example, if it was a toothpaste commercial, the message would be that if you brushed your teeth with this product, your teeth would be whiter, and people would want to have sex with you. If it was a tire commercial, the message was that if you put this tire on your car, your car would have tires that provided a safe, comfortable ride, which would cause people to want to have sex with you. And so on. But then in 1971, Coca-Cola came out with this commercial wherein an extremely multicultural group of attractive young people stood on the side of a scenic hill and sang:

I'd like to teach the world to sing
In perfect harmony
I'd like to buy the world a Coke
And keep it company.

In the troubled times that were the early 1970s, this commercial was so upbeat, so hopeful, so optimistic, so positive, so *happy,* that you could not watch it without wanting to puke. I mean, come ON: I'd like to *buy the world a Coke*??? This was a transparently scummy attempt to link a product to, and thus cash in on, the genuine public hunger for an end to war and strife by suggesting, preposterously, that there was some connection between peace and the consumption of a nutrition-free beverage. This technique was so obnoxious that the rest of the advertising world immediately started copying it, and it is still used today in a wide variety of smarmy commercials in which the viewer sees a series of images of happy people while a Michael Bolton–style singer hyperdramatically wails semi-unintelligible greeting card–style lyrics suggesting that the ultimate source of human happiness is cotton fabrics or Hoover vacuum cleaners. This is just SO misleading. The ultimate source of human happiness is not now, has never been, and never will be, a consumer product. Unless you count beer.

So 1971 was a very, very bad year for trends. But there were several positive developments: On TV, *All in the Family* started its hugely successful run, during which millions of viewers faithfully tuned in each week to laugh at the ignorant, prejudiced rantings of Archie Bunker. Although I suspect that part of the show's appeal was that a lot of these viewers agreed with Archie.

Another highlight of 1971 was that astronaut Alan Shepard hit a golf ball on the Moon. I believe that, for many Americans, this has been the highlight of the entire space program to date, because we could see a direct, practical benefit of space travel: You can hit a *hell* of a golf shot. I think our space program would be WAY more popular today if our astronauts had spent less time on boring, incomprehensible experiments involving frog embryos, and more time doing cool demonstrations of practical benefits ("Today we're going to see what happens when we eject Richard Simmons into open space stark naked").

Finally, 1971 was the year when the first electronic calculators became available to consumers. This was important because, before 1971, you had to remember how to add, subtract, multiply, and divide for your whole lifetime. But with calculators, everybody was free to forget these things, so that now, when you make a purchase, and the amount you owe is $6.38, and you give the cashier a $10 bill, both you and the cashier are totally dependent on the electronic cash register to tell you how much change you should get. It could come up with any random number between $2.13 and $17.94, and both humans involved would unquestioningly accept it. This is only one of the benefits of living in a technologically advanced society.

1972

This was the year when Henry Kissinger announced to a war-weary nation that "Peace is at hand." So naturally it was not. But things were improving elsewhere on the godless Communist front. President Nixon visited both China *and* Russia to sign important agreements and hold formal dinners and exchange high-level ceremonial gifts. Dick gave the Chinese— get ready—a pair of musk oxen.

This has always struck me as a weird gift idea, verging on being a prank. I mean, we are talking about a large, hairy, bulk-pooping animal that gets its name from the fact that it emits a strong and not particularly pleasant odor. This is not an animal that you keep around the executive mansion for companionship. ("Here, boy . . . NO! *NOT SO CLOSE!*") It would not surprise me to learn that, the instant Dick left China, the Chinese converted their ceremonial gift into muskburgers.

But if our official gift *was* intended as a prank, the Chinese definitely got the better of us, because they gave Dick a pair of godless pandas, Hsing-Hsing and Ling-Ling.[5] They were brought to the National Zoo[6] in Washington, D.C., and immediately became major celebrities, along the lines of the Jackson 5. For approximately the next decade the American public and news media were obsessed with the question of when Hsing-Hsing and Ling-Ling would produce a baby.

Unfortunately, for some biological reason it turned out to

---

5. Their names are literally translated as "Chad" and "Jeremy."
6. No, not Congress. The *other* national zoo.

be more likely that the Jackson 5 would produce a live panda offspring than that Hsing-Hsing and Ling-Ling would. My personal theory was that the Chinese deliberately gave Dick two male pandas. But whatever the problem was, American productivity sank lower and lower as we devoted more and more of our national energy to getting Hsing-Hsing and Ling-Ling to produce a new little thing-thing. How bad did it get? Here is a quote, which I swear I am not making up, from a United Press International story that appeared in 1983, by which time the nation had spent *more than ten years* trying to get Hsing-Hsing and Ling-Ling to reproduce: "Dr. John Knight, a London Zoo veterinarian, flew to Washington yesterday afternoon, bringing frozen panda semen."

Today, of course, with our strict antiterrorist airport security procedures, you would not be able to bring something like that onboard a commercial aircraft without first answering some tough questions from the airline ticket agent, such as:

- "Was this semen given to you by a panda or pandas unknown to you?"
- "May I see a photo ID of the panda?"

But getting back to 1972: We also had a presidential election that year. The Republicans of course nominated Dick, whose campaign theme was that he did not have time for politics because he was too busy being a World Leader doing high-level statesperson things such as turning over ceremonial musk oxen to the Chinese.

The Democrats nominated George McGovern, who, knowing he had a tough uphill fight, immediately began, in the time-honored Democratic tradition, screwing up. He selected as his running mate Missouri Senator Thomas Eagleton, who instantly became a major liability when it was reported that he had been hospitalized for depression. This is the kiss of death in American politics. The voters do not want their politicians seeking psychiatric treatment; the voters prefer to have their politicians work out their psychiatric problems in office.

So McGovern, after firmly declaring that he would not dump Eagleton, dumped Eagleton. Then he had to conduct an embarrassing search for a replacement vice presidential candidate, a search in which he was rejected by the top Democrats, the mid-level Democrats, several deceased Democrats, and four of the Jackson 5 before he was finally forced to settle for a man whose name was well-enough known, but who was hardly a political heavyweight: Buffalo Bob.

McGovern got smushed in the election, and Nixon, with the war looking as though it might finally be over next year for real and the Cold War starting to thaw, was poised to go down in history as a Great President. Oh, sure, there was this pesky news story about some bumbling guys breaking into the Democratic national headquarters at the Watergate; there were allegations that these guys were connected to the Nixon campaign, maybe the White House. But few people believed those allegations. It seemed impossible that a president of the United States, especially one as shrewd as Dick, could be involved in anything that *stupid.* So nobody was taking this story seriously except for a couple of reporters at the *Washington Post.* It was pretty much ignored by the rest of the media, including me.

I was in the media at this point, working in West Chester, Pennsylvania, as a reporter for a daily local newspaper called (really) *The Daily Local News.* I was writing obituaries, going to fires, covering school board meetings wherein the board members could take up to two hours just to agree on what day it was. I was writing lengthy, passionate stories about sewage treatment and many other subjects I knew nothing about, which is okay because I seriously doubt that anybody ever read these stories. I was writing my first humor columns.[7] I was balancing a checkbook, paying rent, paying taxes, making payments on a car, and starting to think about the warning signs of gum disease.

In other words, I was making the slow but inevitable transition from Young Person to Adult. Millions of Boomers were doing the same thing, and as they did, the last of the energy was seeping out of The Sixties' counterculture, most obviously on the music scene. The Byrds broke up, and so did Creedence Clearwater Revival and Steppenwolf. To replace their music, we got songs like "Alone Again (Naturally)," "Candy Man," "Song Sung Blue," and "Baby Don't Get Hooked on Me." More weenie music.

The rock 'n' roll well, having flowed so freely for almost a decade, was starting another dry spell. And so, not surprisingly, this was the era that saw the invention of the "oldies" radio format, in which stations played a limited selection of Sixties hits over and over and over, year after year; some stations are still playing them today. This popular format enabled us Boomers, as we grew older, to completely miss most of the later develop-

---

7. Today, when I look back on those old columns, they seem crude and sophomoric. Of course, so do the columns I wrote last month. It's my genre!

ments in popular music. We wrapped ourselves in a comfortable cocoon of sounds from our youth, and thus deluded ourselves into thinking, long after we had entered old-farthood, that we were still cool, singing along to the Dave Clark Five, while in the back seats of our minivans, our kids snickered at us.

1973

This was the year the war finally ended. Nixon called it "peace with honor," although he surely knew that the Communists would take over, just the same as if we had never gotten involved over there in the first place—except of course for the hundreds of thousands of people who got hurt or killed. So you tell me why the whole damned thing was not a terrible, criminal waste. You tell me why Henry Kissinger got the Nobel Peace Prize, instead of being required—along with all the other "leaders" who kept sending Americans over there long after they knew the war was pointless—to get down on his knees and beg the forgiveness of the American veterans, and their families, and the Vietnamese people.

Everybody knew that "peace with honor" was bullshit, but nobody cared at that point. Everybody just wanted it to be *over*. When it finally was, there was no joy, only relief.

It should have been a triumphant year for Dick Nixon, and it would have been, except for the fact that his top administration officials were getting indicted so fast that he was forced to replace them by grabbing individuals virtually at random. (At one point I believe David Eisenhower was attorney general.)

Dick's problem was of course the Watergate scandal, which was turning out to be something after all. A Senate committee started looking into it, and the hearings became one of the most popular shows on television. Millions of us tuned in to hear about the fascinating behind-the-scenes activities of John Dean, H. R. Haldeman, John Ehrlichman, John Mitchell, and other important, powerful, suit-wearing men who had seemed, from the outside, to be so serious, so *official*—but who, as it gradually became clear, had spent much of the previous year scurrying around trying to implement complex, wacky schemes hatched by a president who had transformed, under the pressure of his own paranoia, into Commander Froot Loop.

"I am not a crook," he declared, thereby convincing many that he was.

Needless to say, I, the eager young journalist, ate all of this up. Lowly newspaper reporters, bringing down a corrupt president! We at *The Daily Local News* basked in the reflected glory of Woodward and Bernstein; we were inspired by them; we kept a sharp eye out for any hint of corruption in the way our local school board purchased clarinets for the marching band.

It was a great time to be in the news media, because the news media were widely perceived by the public as the good guys. Of course, that is no longer the case: The public currently ranks the news media, on the ethics scale, down with lawyers, car sellers, politicians, and parasites of the bowel.

But the Watergate era was glorious, especially for print journalists. A wave of idealistic Boomers got into the newspaper business back then. They were going to Uncover the

Truth, Fight for Justice, and Change the World. Today, most of those who remain in the business have risen to management positions and spend their time in lengthy meetings discussing issues such as what page the crossword puzzle should go on.

Anyway, getting back to 1973: As if Watergate wasn't scandal enough for the Nixon administration, Vice President Weasel—Mr. Law and Order—resigned under threat of trial and jail. He was replaced by Gerald Ford, who was generally viewed as a nice man, although not necessarily the sharpest overall dart in the board. He went on to serve as president for roughly twenty-five minutes, after which he spent a couple of decades of dedicated and unselfish involvement with a broad array of distinguished golf tournaments.

Actually, I have fond feelings toward Gerald Ford, largely because of a semi-encounter I had with him in 1995, when he was in his eighties. We had both given speeches at an event in Bakersfield, California, and we were both among the passengers aboard a small, two-propeller commercial plane headed for Los Angeles, where most of us were making connections. The flight was running late, and although everybody was anxious to get going, we figured we had no choice but to first sit through the safety lecture from the co-pilot.

"Ladies and gentlemen," he began, "I'd like to take just a few minutes to . . ."

"Let's just go!" snapped Gerald Ford, former president of the United States.

"Okay, sir!" said the co-pilot, sitting down immediately.

That is my kind of leadership.

1974

For most of the year, Watergate consumed the nation's attention: Virtually everybody was reading transcripts of our chief executive—the president of the United States!—and his henchpersons sitting around the Oval Office plotting obstructions of justice, cursing incessantly, and at times babbling like deranged men. The scandal got so bad that even Dick Nixon seemed embarrassed by it. Facing impeachment, he resigned in August, thus ending what I consider to be the highest-quality presidential administration of my lifetime, as measured by entertainment value. Humor columnists everywhere went into mourning.

So Gerald Ford became president, and he selected, as his vice president, Nelson Rockefeller, whose most memorable act in office was to flip the bird at a heckler on-camera. Other key accomplishments of the Ford administration were:

- **The "WIN" Button.** This was a button that said "WIN," which stood for "Whip Inflation Now!" The plan was that we would all wear these buttons, and this would cause inflation to go away. Incredibly, this plan did not work.
- **Swine-Flu Shots.** These were shots that we were all supposed to get to prevent us from catching Swine Flu, a disease that was threatening to become an epidemic, according to the Ford administration, which was acting on information apparently obtained from a fortune cookie. Most people did not get the shots, which turned

out to be a good thing, because in quite a few cases the shots caused very serious side effects, which resulted in the government having to pay out millions of dollars to victims. Meanwhile, hardly anybody got Swine Flu. Maybe this was because of inflation.

There were a couple of major national fads in 1974: One was "streaking," in which people—usually (surprise!) college students—took off their clothes and sprinted naked through some public place or event. I thought this was a fairly entertaining fad and would like to see it brought back, although if any nostalgic Boomers plan to participate, there should definitely be a weight limitation.

The other big 1974 fad was citizens band, or CB, radio. It was huge; millions of us installed these radios in our cars. We all developed southern accents and spoke in the lingo of the guys who drive the big trucks (or "eighteen-wheelers"), telling each other where the police (or "Smokeys") were using radar (or "taking pictures"). The problem was, for your CB radio to be useful, it had to be on all the time, which meant that you were always listening to the incessant babbling of all the other people who bought CB radios, and many of these people were intellectually unremarkable (or "morons"). So after a few months many of us ultimately decided it was better to just go ahead and get speeding tickets.

The big book in 1974 was *Jaws*, which many people foolishly read while vacationing at the seashore. With each turn of the page, they moved their beach towels farther from the water; some of them wound up as far inland as Kansas.

Speaking of alarming things: It is a scientific fact that 1974 was the worst year in world history for rock music. And I am NOT saying this because among the top musical acts to emerge that year were both Abba AND Barry Manilow. I am saying it because the hit songs included "Kung Fu Fighting," "Seasons in the Sun," "Billy Don't Be a Hero," "The Night Chicago Died," and "(You're) Having My Baby." You could not turn on your radio that year without hearing one of these songs. And yet the Federal Communications Commission did *nothing*.

In the media, the most significant development of 1974 was, I think, the launching of *People* magazine. This marked the beginning of a trend that grew and grew, and still runs strong in America—the public fascination, even obsession, with celebrities; and the corresponding decline of public interest in The Issues. In subsequent decades, the public would become way less interested in the federal budget, and way more interested in Marla Maples.

Maybe this trend got started because, after all the turmoil of The Sixties and early Seventies, people were sick of being depressed by issues. Maybe it was because—with the war over, and Watergate winding down, and the civil rights movement having moved off the streets and into the courts and legislatures—there didn't seem to *be* any compelling issues.[8] Maybe people just got more shallow.

Whatever it was, you could feel the seismic shift in the national mood in the mid-Seventies, especially among the Boomers, who were thinking less and less about saving

---

8. Unless you count the environment, which I agree is extremely important, but which is also, let's be honest, boring, and if you don't believe me, ask Al Gore.

the world, and more and more about attaining personal grati-
fication, by which I mean money. Also, they were starting to
have babies, and, as the old saying goes, "You can't save the
world while a tiny person is throwing up on your shoulder."

And so by 1974 the times—at least the ones Bob Dylan had
been singin' about—had pretty much finished a-changin'.
That's why I am hereby declaring 1974 as the end of the Formative Boomer Years, and I'm going to halt this year-by-year
summary of events. As far as I'm concerned, most of the last
couple of decades are just one big blur anyway; what, really, is
the difference between, say, 1985 and 1987?

Of course one reason I say this is that I'm turning into an
old person, and old people always think there was something
special about the time of their youth. But I think that, if you
lived through the early Boomer years, especially The Sixties,
you have to admit that, as an era, it was a lot more . . . *intense*
than the one we're living in now.

This was not necessarily good. As I said earlier, a lot of what
defined The Sixties was bad. But it *was* intense, and it left us
Boomers feeling a close connection with something bigger
than us, something *historic*.

Of course, our parents' generation has the same kind of
feeling about World War II. The difference is that was a cause
in which almost everybody in America, young and old, was on
the same side; it drew the generations, the nation, closer
together. Whereas we Boomers found ourselves in conflict,
occasionally violent conflict, with our own government, our
own culture, our own parents. And in some of those conflicts,
we turned out to be right.

We came out of that era mistrustful, even disdainful, of our elders; we were also more than a little smug. We are still that way.[9] Whatever we get into—having careers, raising kids, dieting, exercising, discovering spirituality, growing old—we tend to make a big deal about doing it our own way, which we insist is a smarter and better way, because the old ways are not good enough for us. We also tend to think—because there are so many of us, and because we were spoiled rotten as children—that whatever life phase we happen to be going through is society's most critical concern. For these reasons (and others, such as our "oldies" music) the generations before and after us—and I don't blame them one bit—tend to think we're self-centered, overbearing, and tiresome.

We are the big fat loudmouth of generations. I accept that. But . . .

But my generation is a LOT less likely to let the government draft our sons and send them off to fight, without really knowing why, than my parents' generation was. We are also less likely (though not *enough* less likely) to laugh at racist jokes.

I also believe that, even though we Boomers are not the best order-followers, we turned out—when we finally got around to pursuing careers—to be pretty hard workers. We have not necessarily been competent parents, but we are loving, and we are capable of making an honest effort to understand why one of our offspring might want to wear a ring in his or her eyelid. We are no longer capable of being hip, but by endlessly *aspiring* to be hip, by *encouraging* hipness, we have

---

9. You may feel that these are gross generalizations. Too bad.

enabled America to lead the world in that category. We usually signal our turns. We don't take too many things too seriously. We forgive a lot, because we've *done* a lot. We get up and dance at wedding receptions. And, dammit, our music *was* better than most of the dreck that followed.

A few years ago I got into a heated argument with the 18-year-old son of a friend of mine. Actually, it wasn't so much an argument as it was me getting angry at him for something he said. What he said, basically, was that he wished there was a war like Vietnam going on right then, so that the members of his generation would have something big, something exciting, in their lives. I told him that this was a reprehensible thing to say; I told him he should not want people to die to keep his generation amused.

But in retrospect—although I obviously don't want another Vietnam—I see what he meant. He didn't want people to die; he wanted there to be something to give his life significance, something to mark his formative era that would be more meaningful than whatever TV sitcoms were popular at the time. We Boomers had that; we had a *lot* going on, maybe too much.

On balance, though, I'm glad I went through it. I think most of us are. We have a bond, us Boomers. We've been through all *kinds* of stuff together, and it's all still with us, defining us—the Bomb, the Hula Hoop, the godless Communists, Elvis, the Kennedy Assassination, the Beatles, Vietnam, protests, drugs, moon walks, Woodstock, Watergate—all still in our brains, swirling around and around . . .

At the center, of course, is Buffalo Bob.

Discussion Questions—The Early Seventies

Can you name three more bad songs from 1974? I can: "I Honestly Love You," "Band on the Run," and "I Shot the Sheriff."

Do people who wear bicycle shorts have any idea how they look?

What was your CB "handle"? You will never guess mine. (Hint: Bull Fiddle.)

6

An Invitation to Boomers Reaching 50:

Unite! You Have Nothing to Lose But... But...

Shoot, I Forgot What You Have to Lose.

Many bad things happen when you turn 50. You can't see; you can't hear; you can read the entire *Oxford English Dictionary* in the time it takes you to go to the bathroom; and you keep meeting people *your own age* who look like Grandpa Walton.[1]

But none of those is the worst thing. The worst thing is that, soon after your 50th birthday, you get The Letter. You older individuals know what letter I'm talking about: It's the one inviting you to join the AARP, which stands for "American Association of Retired Persons Who Are Always Ahead of You in Line Asking if They Get a Discount."

AARP is a large and powerful organization, similar to the

---

1. And those are the *women*.

Mafia but more concerned about dietary fiber. AARP is greatly feared in Washington, D.C., because of the fierce way it lobbies for issues of concern to senior citizens, such as Social Security, Medicare, and the constitutional right to drive without any clue where the actual road is. Whenever Congress is considering legislation that in any way affects these programs, AARP sends trained commando squadrons of elderly people to visit the congresspersons who disagree with the official AARP position. If these congresspersons do not change their minds, their bodies are later found bound hand and foot with support stockings, their skin covered with ugly round welts from being viciously jabbed with cane tips.

So, AARP is not an organization to mess with. And when you reach 50, no matter where you are, AARP tracks you down and sends you the invitation letter.

"Dear Old Fart," it begins.

No, it doesn't really. But it might as well. Because if you're like me—that is, if you still find yourself wondering what you're going to do when you grow up—it comes as a shock to be formally invited to join a group of retired persons.[2]

My letter was signed by the executive director, Horace B. Deets,[3] which is the perfect name for the executive director of

---

2. Interestingly, the AARP invitation states: "YOU NEED NOT BE RETIRED," which is kind of an unusual thing for an association of retired persons to say. Nevertheless I admire this spirit of openmindedness, and would like to see it extended to other organizations such as the American Medical Association ("YOU NEED NOT KNOW ANYTHING ABOUT MEDICINE") or the priesthood ("YOU NEED NOT BELIEVE IN A SUPREME BEING") or the U.S. House of Representatives ("YOU NEED NOT BE A MONEY-GRUBBING HYPOCRITE").

3. You probably already know this, but "Horace B. Deets" can be rearranged to spell "He-Cat Bedsore."

AARP. If your name is Horace, even when you're very young, you are clearly destined for a career in the retirement field. I bet when Horace was a baby and his grandparents dandled him on their knees they told him: "Horace, someday you're going to grow up and retire!"

But I'm not named Horace, and I'm not at *all* comfortable with the concept of being a Retired Person. I don't mean the part about not working. I could adjust to that. I mean the part about joining an organization whose membership includes many men—as a resident of South Florida, I see these men all the time—who pull the waist of their pants up to their armpits, perhaps so that, in case of emergency, you could perform open-heart surgery on them by unzipping the fly.

There's nothing *wrong* with this look; it's just not *my* look. Gosh darn it, I'm a Boomer! We Boomers have, for decades, consoled ourselves with the thought that, even though we're getting relentlessly older, and we're definitely nowhere near as cool as our kids, at least we're still cooler than *somebody*, and that somebody has always been the people in the generations ahead of us. We can look ourselves in the mirror and say, "Okay, maybe I'm starting to *resemble* Lawrence Welk, but at least I never liked his *music*." We Boomers may have abandoned all our other principles, but we cannot, just because we're reaching 50, abandon what tiny shreds of coolness superiority we have left and join the High-Pants People.

So I am not going to join AARP. I am, instead, going to start a new organization, which will be called BARF, which stands for "Boomers Against Reaching Farthood." Here is the:

OFFICIAL CHARTER
BOOMERS AGAINST REACHING FARTHOOD
(BARF)

MEMBERSHIP REQUIREMENTS

Membership in BARF is restricted to those people who, when somebody says to them, "People try to put us down," immediately and involuntarily respond, "Just because we get around."

WHAT BARF DOES

BARF monitors its members for the common warning signs of incipient farthood, such as:

- Wearing white shoes.
- Repeatedly telling the same anecdote about something that happened thirty-seven years ago and wasn't even interesting then.
- Wearing a hat.
- Collecting ceramic cats.
- When children call or visit, spending the entire conversation whining at them for never calling or visiting.
- Putting any kind of clothing on a dog or any other animal that already *has* fur, for God's sake.
- Wearing knee socks.
- Becoming involved with organized Bingo.
- At restaurants, always insisting on separate checks and using discount coupons and calling the waitperson over every twenty-five seconds and leaving a 9 percent tip and just generally turning the process of dining out into a hellish experience that is far more complex and hostile than the Middle East peace talks.
- Purchasing any form of Oldsmobile.

If a BARF member starts exhibiting any of this type of behavior, BARF will send out a Crisis Intervention Team to confront the member, and if necessary lock him or her in a motel room and make him or her watch a videotape of *Animal House* until he or she has regressed far enough on the aging scale to rejoin normal human society. (The only exception will be if the member is wearing both white shoes AND knee socks, in which case the Crisis Intervention Team will simply shoot the member in the head.)

MEMBER DISCOUNT PROGRAM

When you join BARF, you will receive an official membership card. If you show this card at any one of thousands of participating business establishments throughout the United States and ask for a "senior" discount, you will be asked to leave.

LOBBYING ACTIVITIES

To represent you, its membership, BARF will employ a team of highly paid lobbyists in Washington, D.C. These lobbyists will not go to hearings, nor will they issue position statements, nor will they take members of Congress to dinner. They will, in fact, never go anywhere near the organized federal government. "Issues, Schmissues" will be their official motto. What the BARF lobbyists *will* do, on your behalf, is party. They will party constantly and with great rowdiness, so that you, as a BARF member, will have the satisfaction of saying to yourself: "Perhaps I am unable to personally go to Washington and get tanked and annoy people and wind up dancing stark naked in the Jefferson Memorial, but at least I know that trained professionals are doing this for me!" Your BARF lobbyists will be so active that when the citizens of Washington hear screams, loud explosions, or the sound of cattle being driven through the streets, they will not even bother to look out the window. They will just say: "It's BARF! Lock the doors!" That is the level of clout that you will have in our nation's capital.

HEALTH COUNSELING HOTLINE

Aging people have many special health problems. As a member of BARF, if you want to talk about your medical situation, but cannot find a "sympathetic ear" to listen, you can call a special toll-free Health Counseling Hotline, any hour of the day or night, 365 days a year, and hear a recorded message counseling you that nobody wants to hear about your medical situation.

OFFICIAL MEMBERSHIP CARD

Without question the single most tangible benefit of joining BARF is that you get to carry the prestigious BARF membership card. To obtain yours, you must undergo the rigorous Membership Verification Process, which involves cutting out the following rectangle.[4]

---

4. Note that cutting the page will permanently damage this book. So you will want to purchase another one.

OFFICIAL MEMBERSHIP CARD

This card, when placed in a qualified wallet, serves as proof that

(YOUR NAME)

is a qualified member of

BARF

BOOMERS AGAINST REACHING FARTHOOD

and should be asked to leave if he or she asks for a "Senior"

discount. Also, do NOT sell this person a hat.

7
Tips on Looking Young

Fact: Dick Clark Actually Died in 1972.

I don't want to sound conceited, but for a 50-year-old man, I look very young. On more than one occasion, I have been mistaken for a man of 48. (As it happens, that man was wanted by the authorities for bombing a post office, but still, I was flattered.)

When I go out in public, I often notice that people are studying my facial skin closely.

"Your face," they say, haltingly. "It has a . . . a . . ."

"A silky smoothness and youthful glow?" I answer, knowingly.

"No, a piece of Cheez-It stuck to it," they say.

This is jealousy on their part. What they really want to say is: "Dave, you have such a youthful appearance! I wish you would reveal your secrets!"

Okay, then. The first, and most important, thing that you must do if you want to look young is:

1. Delay Puberty for as Long as Possible.

I myself waited until I was approximately 25 years old. At least that's how it seems to me now, looking back on my youth, especially the critical junior high school years, which were no picnic. I was totally betrayed by my friends. We had all been, biologically, boys for as long as I could remember, and then, one fateful day, without telling me, they all sneaked off for a big shopping spree at the Hormone Store, and suddenly they started turning into *men*, becoming larger and deeper-voiced and hairier right before my eyes, similar to werewolves, but with more acne.

And of course the junior high girls were going through even more extreme changes. I'd see a girl in a morning math class, and she'd look basically the way she'd looked all through elementary school; and then that very afternoon, the same girl would walk into American history class, and she'd be . . . a *woman*, with makeup and stockings and bazooms and everything, and she'd already be dating a commercial airline pilot.

So the girls were becoming women, and the boys were becoming men, and I was becoming obsessed with my armpits. My thinking was that, if I was going to develop bodily hair, this is the first place it would sprout. I spent a lot of time locked in the bathroom, holding my arms over my head and scrutinizing my pits for signs of fuzz. This is what I was doing when Al Gore was running for student council.

In other words, adolescence was not a good time for me. It was during this phase of my life that I developed into a class clown; in fact, I went on to be formally elected Class Clown of the Pleasantville High School class of 1965. If you were to do a study of all the people who, in school, were elected Class Clown, you'd find that exactly zero percent of this group was also elected Most Attractive, or even Most Average-Looking. No, we Class Clowns *became* class clowns because we were the unattractive, inadequate, and sometimes hairless individuals who, having been rejected for membership in the National Hormone Society, were forced to develop a sense of humor so that the other students would like us. At parties, when the other students were dancing the Dirty Dog or sneaking off to darkened corners and groping their way around the various bases, we Class Clowns were the ones standing alone, trying to get attention via sight gags involving hors d'oeuvres.

You know what ticks me off? What ticks me off is when women say—and women are *always* saying this—that the quality they find most attractive in the opposite gender is a sense of humor. Whenever we Class Clowns hear that, we emit a bitter, barking laugh, reminiscent of a seal having its prostate examined. We are asking ourselves: *Where were these women when we were standing at the hors d'oeuvres table with carrot sticks in both nostrils?* I'll tell you: They were off in the corner willingly being groped by large, hairy, non-humorous members of the football team.

And please do not even try to tell me that women become more attracted to a sense of humor when they get older. If a stand-up comedian is on TV, and you say something to a woman, she will turn to you and respond. If Brad Pitt is on TV, and you say something to a woman, she may respond to you in a vacant and distracted manner, but she will continue to stare, fish-like, at Brad Pitt. This is true even if the comedian is firing off a string of hilarious jokes, and Brad Pitt is merely standing there with his trademark sultry expression, indicating either yearning sensuousness or volcanic diarrhea.

Here are the names of some other males who (1) are constantly having to check their clothing in case they have to brush off underpants that women have hurled at them; and (2) have never intentionally said anything funny that was not written for them by somebody else:

Tom Cruise
Robert Redford
Denzel Washington
Mel Gibson
Leonardo DiCaprio
John F. Kennedy Jr.
Everybody on *Melrose Place*
Fabio
Bill Clinton

But getting back to my original point, which, as those of you with photographic memories will recall, is puberty. I was a very late bloomer, and this fact made my life quite painful during adolescence, which in my case lasted for several decades. But in the long run, it paid off, because now I look unusually youthful, and many of my peers look like Dwight Eisenhower. And I want to *rub it in.* I want to have a Class of 1965 reunion *right now,* so that I can walk up to some former-stud football player and say: "Hi, I'm Dave Barry! Which class member's father are you?" Ha ha! That would be a good one! I would really enjoy that, until the former-stud football player threatened to punch my face in. Then, to make him see that I was just kidding, I would put carrot sticks up my nose.

My second tip on how to look young is:

2. Get Plenty of Sleep.

When I say "plenty of sleep," I am not talking about eight hours per night. If that's all the sleep you're getting, it's only a matter of time before people start mistaking you for Keith Richards. As an older person, you need to get *as much sleep as you possibly can.* "When the going gets tough, the older person takes a nap," that should be your motto. Why? Because of the following Known Scientific Fact:

 Your body does not age when you are sleeping.

This was proven by the famous medical case study by the esteemed Dr. Irving concerning a subject named Rip Van Winkle, who fell asleep and slept for twenty years, and he *didn't age a single day.* The downside was, he had hallucinations involving bowling elves, but that is a small price to pay for a youthful appearance.

Here's something else to consider: According to FBI statistics, *fewer than 11 percent of all violent crimes* are committed by people who are sleeping.

Yes, sleep is a highly beneficial activity. Yet for some reason, many people frown on sleeping, especially during working hours. When Ronald Reagan was president, people made all kinds of fun of the fact that he preferred not to be awakened for every single little personnel decision or cabinet meeting or nuclear crisis.

So you have to learn to do what many of us have learned to do: lie about napping. I do this all the time. If somebody calls me when I'm asleep in the middle of the day, I sit bolt upright and answer the phone with an extremely—almost violently—perky voice. I sound like a game-show announcer on amphetamines.

"HELLO!" I shout.

"I'm sorry," the caller says. "Were you sleeping?" (For some reason, the caller almost always asks this when I use my perky voice.)

"NO!" I shout, adding, for clarification: "NO!"

"I'll call you back later," the caller says.

"FINE!" I shout. "I WON'T BE SLEEPING THEN, EITHER!"

The problem with this technique is that when the phone wakes me up in the middle of the night, when I have every right to be sound asleep, I find myself automatically lying about it anyway.

"HELLO!" I'll shout into the receiver, sometimes adding for emphasis, "I'M NOT ASLEEP!"

"Why not?" the caller asks. "It's 3:30 A.M."

I hope that, as we Boomers get older and need more sleep, society in general[1] will change its negative stereotyped image of napping and start encouraging it. I think the federal gov-

---

1. You know who you are.

ernment should work on this, instead of nattering on endlessly about issues such as day care. We Boomers don't *want* day care! We want tough Right-To-Nap laws!

It would also help if the people who produce our popular culture[2] would make an effort to portray napping in a positive light. Let's take a standard scene from an action-adventure movie, wherein two ruggedly handsome action heroes discover a bomb with a detonator counting down. Usually the scene goes something like this:

FIRST HERO: Christ, there's enough explosives here to destroy half the city!
SECOND HERO: And the timer says only ninety seconds left!
FIRST HERO: We have to deactivate this thing!
SECOND HERO: But *which wire* do we cut? If we cut the wrong one, it blows right now!
FIRST HERO: We're going to have to guess!
SECOND HERO: Here goes! Wish me luck, buddy!
   (Dramatic music plays as we see the second hero, his face sweating, reaching down to cut one of the wires . . .)

Do you see the problem with this? Do you see how *insensitive* this scene is to aging Baby Boomers? There is no reason why it could not be rewritten as follows:

FIRST HERO: Christ, there's enough explosives here to destroy half the city!

---

2. You know who you are.

SECOND HERO: And the timer says only ninety seconds left!
FIRST HERO: Great! We have time for a brief nap!
SECOND HERO: Good idea! By napping now, we will remain ruggedly handsome that much longer!

(Dramatic music plays as we see the two heroes inflating small portable air mattresses.)

Likewise, in popular music, I see no reason why there could not be more popular songs with titles like "I Really, Really Want to Make Love to You, Baby, So Please Wake Me Up in Two Hours."

And speaking of bad, my third tip for remaining young-looking is:

3. Avoid Medical Care.

Medical care is the number-one cause of sudden rapid aging among middle-aged people. Ask yourself how many times you have heard somebody tell you a story like this: "Ralph was feeling fine, no problems at all, and then he went in for a routine physical checkup, and the next thing we heard he was in critical condition with the majority of his internal organs sitting in a freezer in an entirely different building."

I'm not saying that the medical profession deliberately *tries* to treat apparently healthy people essentially the same way that high school biology students treat frogs. And I am *certainly* not saying that you should refrain from getting needed medical care.[3] I'm simply saying that modern doctors have had many years of training, and they have access to a vast arsenal of miracle drugs and devices and surgical techniques, and by God they are going to use these things on *somebody*. They can't help themselves! It's human nature! They're like a teenage boy who has just been handed the keys to a brand-new Ferrari. He's *not* going to let it just sit in the driveway; he's going to take it out and crash it.

So if you walk into a medical facility for any reason whatsoever, including to fix the photocopier machine, medical professionals are going to pounce on you and remove six quarts of your blood and three to four pounds of tissue, and they will put these things into an extremely sophisticated high-tech diagnostic device that, by processing literally billions of bits of data at lightning speed, will tell them, within a matter of seconds, with a 99.999 percent probability of accuracy, whether or not you have medical insurance.

If you do, they will put you inside a large scary device called a CAT scanner, with "CAT" standing for "Computerized Automatic Thingthatwillfindsomethingwrongwithyounomatterhowgoodyoufeel." The next thing you know, you're strapped to a gurney being wheeled at upwards of thirty miles per hour to the operating room, surrounded by burly nursing personnel who apparently have a side bet going to see who can insert the largest-diameter tube into some orifice of your body. "Nobody Gets Out of Here Without Sutures"—that is the motto of the medical profession.

---

3. I am not saying this because I do not wish to get sued.

My final, and most important, tip for looking young is:

4. Learn to Manage Stress.

Let's say you have a job that carries with it a great deal of stress, as indicated by medical symptoms such as a recurring pain caused by pounding your head against your desk. This is not good. Not only is stress unhealthy; it also causes you to age more rapidly, as was demonstrated by an authoritative 1987 study by the Harvard School of Medicine, which concluded that "in *Snow White and the Seven Dwarfs*, Grumpy looks WAY older than Happy."[4]

So you need to learn to relieve your stress. You must not let it become bottled up inside, where it can cause harm to you; you must let it out, where it can cause harm to others.

Let's say you're a customer-service representative, and you're on the phone with a typical member of the public, by which I mean an individual who has the cognitive powers of celery. Let's say this person is complaining vehemently and rudely about a problem that probably does not exist, and is demanding that you do something about it. From a stress-management perspective, there is a right way and a wrong way to handle this situation:

HIGH-STRESS APPROACH: "I'm sorry you're having trouble with our product. Let me take down some information that will help me assist you."

---

4. There *was* a dwarf named "Happy," right?

STRESS-MANAGEMENT APPROACH: "I'm sorry you're having trouble with our product. Why don't you stick it up your butt?"

Obviously, you can't use exactly this technique in every situation. If you were, for example, a negotiator in the Middle East Peace talks, you'd have to modify the wording ("Why don't you stick it up your butt, Your Excellency?").

You can also reduce stress by using a breathing technique developed over the centuries by Hindu mystics, and practiced today by millions of Americans enrolled in yoga classes. Basically, what you do is take a deep breath, then exhale slowly while saying: "I quit this stupid class! I'm going to have a beer!"

If these tips don't make you look as young as you would like, there is always the fast-growing field of cosmetic surgery. More and more Baby Boomers are taking advantage of surgical techniques such as face-lifts to transform themselves from people who look as if they're in their late 40s or early 50s into people who look like the intelligent reptile aliens on *Star Trek: The Next Generation.*

Another problem is that the body parts that have been operated on often don't seem to go with the ones that haven't. I once sat at a formal dinner with a woman who was around 60, except for her breasts, which were maybe six months old. You could get a good look at them because the woman was wearing a dress that was so low cut that her shoes were sticking out the top. "Take a look at my new breasts!" was the message she was sending via this dress. And I suppose they were perfectly fine breasts, taken individually, but they were about two feet apart, and neither one of them seemed to have anything in common with the rest of the woman. She would have looked just as natural with, say, a pair of ferrets sticking out of her dress.

Yes, it can be pretty silly, the extremes to which some aging people will go in an effort to look younger. So don't get hung up on it. Don't be victimized by our shallow, youth-obsessed culture. Don't start believing that you're unattractive just because you're developing gray hair and wrinkles and big hideous spots all over your body. You look fine! Really! And I'm not just being patronizing because, as I mentioned earlier, I happen to be unusually youthful-looking. I'm sure I'll feel exactly the same unconcerned way when I start to look old. I'll just look myself in the mirror, and I'll say: "You're getting older! It's a natural part of life, and it's okay!"

Then I'll shoot the mirror.

8

25 Things
I Have Learned in 50 Years

1. The badness of a movie is directly proportional to the number of helicopters in it.

* * *

2. You will never find anybody who can give you a clear and compelling reason why we observe "Daylight Saving Time."

* * *

3. People who feel the need to tell you that they have an excellent sense of humor are telling you that they have no sense of humor.

* * *

4. The most valuable function performed by the federal government is entertainment.

* * *

5. You should never say anything to a woman that even remotely suggests you think she's pregnant unless you can see an actual baby emerging from her at that moment.

* * *

6. A penny saved is worthless.

* * *

7. They can hold all the peace talks they want, but there will never be peace in the Middle East. Billions of years from now, when Earth is hurtling toward the Sun and there is nothing left alive on the planet except a few microorganisms, the microorganisms living in the Middle East will be bitter enemies.

* * *

8. The most powerful force in the universe is: gossip.

* * *

9. The one thing that unites all human beings, regardless of age, gender, religion, economic status, or ethnic background, is that, deep down inside, we all believe that we are above-average drivers.

* * *

10. There comes a time when you should stop expecting other people to make a big deal about your birthday. That time is: age 11.

* * *

11. There is a very fine line between "hobby" and "mental illness."

* * *

12. People who want to share their religious views with you almost never want you to share yours with them.

* * *

13. There apparently exists, somewhere in Los Angeles, a computer that generates concepts for television sitcoms.

When TV executives need a new concept, they turn on this computer; after sorting through millions of possible plot premises, it spits out, "THREE QUIRKY BUT ATTRACTIVE YOUNG PEOPLE LIVING IN AN APART-MENT," and the executives turn this concept into a show. The next time they need an idea, the computer spits out, "SIX QUIRKY BUT ATTRACTIVE YOUNG PEOPLE LIVING IN AN APARTMENT." Then the next time, it spits out, "FOUR QUIRKY BUT ATTRACTIVE YOUNG PEOPLE LIVING IN AN APARTMENT." And so on. We need to locate this computer and destroy it with hammers.

* * *

14. Nobody is normal.

* * *

15. At least once per year, some group of scientists will become very excited and announce that:
    • The universe is *even bigger* than they thought!
    • There are *even more* subatomic particles than they thought!
    • Whatever they announced last year about global warming is wrong.

* * *

16. If you had to identify, in one word, the reason why the human race has not achieved, and never will achieve, its full potential, that word would be: "meetings."

* * *

17. The main accomplishment of almost all organized protests is to annoy people who are not in them.

* * *

18. The value of advertising is that it tells you the exact opposite of what the advertiser actually thinks. For example:

    •If the advertisement says "This is not your father's Oldsmobile," the advertiser is desperately concerned that this Oldsmobile, like all other Oldsmobiles, appeals primarily to old farts like your father.

    •If Coke and Pepsi spend billions of dollars to convince you that there are significant differences between these two products, both companies realize that Pepsi and Coke are virtually identical.

    •If the advertisement strongly suggests that Nike shoes enable athletes to perform amazing feats, Nike wants you to disregard the fact that shoe brand is unrelated to athletic ability.

    •If Budweiser runs an elaborate advertising campaign stressing the critical importance of a beer's "born-on" date, Budweiser knows this factor has virtually nothing to do with how good a beer tastes.

    •If an advertisement shows a group of cool, attractive youngsters getting excited and high-fiving each other because the refrigerator contains Sunny Delight, the advertiser knows that any real youngster who reacted in this way to this beverage would be considered by his peers to be the world's biggest dipshit.

    And so on. On those rare occasions when advertising dares to poke fun at the product—as in the classic Volkswagen Beetle campaign—it's because the advertiser actually thinks the product is pretty good. If a politician ever ran for president under a slogan such as "Harlan Frubert: Basically, He Wants Attention," I would quit my job to work for his campaign.

* * *

19. If there really is God who created the entire universe with all of its glories, and He decides to deliver a message to humanity, He will not use, as His messenger, a person on cable TV with a bad hairstyle.

* * *

20. You should not confuse your career with your life.

* * *

21. A person who is nice to you, but rude to the waiter, is not a nice person.

* * *

22. No matter what happens, somebody will find a way to take it too seriously.

* * *

23. When trouble arises and things look bad, there is always one individual who perceives a solution and is willing to take command. Very often, that individual is crazy.

* * *

24. Your friends love you anyway.

* * *

25. Nobody cares if you can't dance well. Just get up and dance.

9
Sending Your Child
to College

Remember: You Don't Need Both of Your Kidneys.

As a parent, one of your most important responsibilities is to help get your child through college. Without a college education, your child will enter the job market with no useful skills; whereas *with* a college education, your child will enter the job market with no useful skills and parents who are hundreds of thousands of dollars in debt.

Yes, college is very expensive, and it's getting more so every year, as we can see from this chart:[1]

---

1. *Source:* The Hunchback of Notre Dame.

AVERAGE COST OF FOUR YEARS OF COLLEGE

When You Went to College	$14,340
Today	$343,768
Projected Cost by the Time Your Youngest Child Enters College	ONE BAJILLION DOLLARS (Not including snacks)

Perhaps you're wondering why college costs are skyrocketing, especially considering that (a) inflation has been low; and (b) college mainly consists of students trying to stay awake while listening to assistant professors drone away on topics that will never be of any earthly use to anybody who does not intend to become an assistant professor.

Well, for your information, Mr. or Ms. Skeptical, it takes *a lot of money* to operate a college these days. The costs include:

• Salaries for full professors, who are paid a lot better than assistant professors, even though nobody has ever actually seen one.
• Those comical hats the faculty members wear at graduation.
• The many expenses associated with operating a truly professional football team.

- The cost of producing a promotional film to show at halftime when your football team plays on TV, depicting a racially diverse group of students engaging in typical academic activities—frowning through microscopes, frowning at computers, frowning at the insides of dead rats, etc.—while a deep-voiced professional announcer says something like: "Southwest North Central Louisiana Agricultural, Mechanical and Botanical— where the leaders of tomorrow are vomiting out of the dormitory windows today."
- Huge printing and postage costs for mass mailings to alert the alumni which of them are dead and ask the remaining ones for more money.

There are many additional reasons why college is so expensive. To name just one: A number of leading colleges and universities have started generating their own electricity using turbines powered by steam that is heated by setting fire to huge piles of $50 bills.

"It's a lot of work," explains the president of the Association of University Administrators, "but it's the only way we've been able to keep our costs skyrocketing during this extended period of low inflation."

The point is, you need to be thinking about which college your child is going to attend, and how you're going to pay for it. You should start by taking this:

Survey for Parents of College-Bound Children

In each of the following categories, circle the phrase that most accurately completes the sentence, and note the number of points:

Academic Record
Your child has:
- Excellent grades (+15 points)
- Average grades (+5 points)
- Below-average grades (−10 points)
- Stabbed several teachers (−30 points)

High School Extracurricular Activities
Your child is:
- President of the Honor Society (+15 points)
- A member of a varsity sports team (+10 points)
- Active in school clubs and organizations (+5 points)
- Thinking of getting a nipple ring (−10 points)

Parental Factors
You:
- Did not attend the college to which your child is applying (−5 points)
- Attended the college, but were asked to leave after the dormitory burned down (−15 points)

• Actually graduated from the college (+10 points)

• Have regularly contributed money to the college (+25 points)

• Have pictures of the college president naked with a Shetland pony (+150 points)

Your Financial Situation

You:

• Have enough money for all college costs (+15 points)

• Will need some financial help (−5 points)

• Eat from Dumpsters (−20 points)

SCORING: Add up your total points, giving yourself a 20-point bonus if the Shetland pony is wearing stockings. To interpret your score, refer to the following table:

Point Total	Type of Institution Your Child Should Be Considering
100 or more	Institutions with ivy on the walls and nicknames like "The Crimson"
50–100	Institutions with paint on the walls and nicknames like "The Horned Mollusks"
0–50	Institutions with graffiti on the walls and nicknames like "The Fighting Appliance Repairpersons"
Below 0	Institutions with armed guards on the walls and nicknames like "The Hole"

Next, by consulting with a trained guidance counselor or flipping a coin, you should select several likely colleges and visit them, ideally with your child. During your visit, you should make a point of attending classes and popping into dormitory rooms unannounced. Feel free to ask questions in a loud nasal voice. Some good ones are:

(In the classroom:)
- "If you're so smart, how come you're just an assistant professor?"
- "Is anybody besides me *bored* by this topic?"

(In the dormitory:)
- "You *like* this music?"
- "So, where do you kids today hide your drugs?"
- "Mind if I look through your drawers?"

Your goal, in asking these questions, is to remind your child how hideously embarrassing you are to be around, so that your child will never ever, no matter what happens, move back in with you after college. In fact many parents, as an extra precaution, enter the Federal Witness Protection Program while their children are away at college.

But the main thing to remember is that in giving your child the precious gift of a college education you are enabling him or her to be exposed to the thinking of the greatest minds that the human race has ever produced—from Socrates to Aristotle to Chaucer to Shakespeare to Jane Austen to Abraham Lincoln to Thomas Edison to Bill Gates. None of whom, for the record, graduated from college.

10
Planning for Your Retirement

A Sensible Proposal

Wouldn't you like to live on "Easy Street"?

Wouldn't you like to have the carefree lifestyle depicted in those TV commercials for Merrill Lynch, the ones featuring retired people who seem to have plenty of money to enjoy the finer things in life—golfing, traveling, beating the servants, etc.?

Did you ever wonder how these people got where they are? Well, there's no mystery to it: They worked hard all their lives, planned ahead, and saved every nickel they could. So when it finally came time to retire, they had a bunch of nickels. This was enough for them to live on for about two weeks, after which they had to come out of retirement and take jobs as actors in Merrill Lynch commercials. When the residuals run out, they'll have to survive by eating dog food.

You might not be so lucky. That's why you need to start planning for your retirement *right now*. First off, you need to prepare a current financial statement. Don't worry if you're not a professional accountant. All you have to do is follow these simple, step by step instructions:

STEP ONE: Gather up all your financial records.
STEP TWO: Get a sheet of paper, and at the top write the words "Financial Statement."
STEP THREE: Give this paper to a professional accountant and say, "Fill this out."

When you get your financial statement, there should be a number at the bottom labeled "Net Worth." Look at this number, and decide which of the following categories you fall into:

CATEGORY ONE: Your net worth is large enough for you to retire comfortably.
CATEGORY TWO: Your net worth is not large enough for you to retire comfortably.
CATEGORY THREE: Your net worth is not there, because the accountant, after examining your records, realized that you don't even have enough money to pay for a financial statement.

Chances are that you fall into one of the latter two categories. It's pathetic, isn't it? All those years of working, and so little to show for it! Think of all the money you wasted over the years on things you clearly, in retrospect, could have done without, such as whiskey and slot machines and your children!

But as the country folk say, after generations of inbreeding,

"There's no use beating a dead horse over spilt milk." So it's time to stop feeling sorry for yourself, and start figuring out how you're going to survive when you get old.

One option, of course, is to keep right on working. Why should you stop leading a productive life just because you reach a certain arbitrary age and have become slow and weak and confused and incapable of performing any task more complex than drooling? In today's job market, there are plenty of enterprises that are looking to hire old, senile workers, including:

- The security-guard industry, which routinely gives loaded firearms to people who can no longer remember how to zip up their pants;
- The United States Senate, where Strom Thurmond was allowed to remain as an active, voting member for at least six years past his death; and
- The Rolling Stones, who currently average 107 years old and must constantly hire new members to replace the ones who keel over onstage.

If you don't want to keep working, you're going to need some source of retirement income. If you work for a company, chances are that it has provided some kind of pension plan to reward you for your years of loyal service. That is the good news. The bad news is, at any moment your company could be acquired by another company, a company that is owned by another company that is owned by another company that is owned by an extremely ruthless entrepreneur who is known on Wall Street as "The Scalpel" and who feels exactly as loyal toward retired employees as he does toward insects in his salad. He will find some way to steal your pension or, worse, he will have your pension plan administered by the same fugitive Nazis who administer your "managed care" health plan, which means the chances that you will ever see any actual money are the same as the chances that you will see a live doctor without first having to sit in a waiting room long enough to memorize every word in the March 1978 issue of *Redbook* magazine provided for your reading enjoyment.

So you can't count on your pension. Of course there is always Social Security. This popular program is basically a sacred covenant between the generations, which works as follows: For your whole working life, you pay in money, which goes to support the older retired generation. Then, when you reach age 65, the older generation will come back out of retirement and support *you.*

No, I'm kidding. The older generation will by that point be mostly employed in the field of decomposition. *Your* Social Security money will have to come from the younger generation. The problem here is that the younger generation—and this is just SO typical of how selfish and thoughtless these modern kids are—is not large enough to support all of us Boomers. For now, Social Security is running a surplus, but our leaders have (surprise!) chosen to spend, rather than save, this extra money. This means that, unless something is done, when huge numbers of us Boomers start to retire and collect Social Security, the whole system will collapse like a Barbie chair under Senator Edward Kennedy. Even as you read these words, your elected representatives in Congress are trying to decide how to solve this problem, which can best be understood by referring to the following chart:

THE SOCIAL SECURITY CRISIS
A Statistical Analysis

Number of Retiring Baby Boomers	Millions
Likelihood that your elected representatives in Washington will make a financially responsible but politically unpopular decision	Zero
Size of federal pension and benefit plans that your elected representatives in Washington have made sure that they will receive even if the entire Social Security system goes down the toilet	Big

When we study this chart closely, we see that the likelihood that we Boomers will be able to depend on Social Security is approximately the same as the likelihood that Bill Clinton and Monica Lewinsky spent their time alone in the Oval Office playing Twister.

So what are we Boomers going to do? How are we going to survive when we're old and poor? Who will take care of us?

I have a solution, which I think is both sensible and fair. I am proposing that when we Boomers retire we move in with the one group of people who owe us the most—the people whom we have generously supported and taken care of; the people for whom we have made tremendous sacrifices all of our adult lives.

No, I'm not talking about moving in with our children. We should not have to spend our golden years listening to rap music. I'm talking about *moving in with retired members of Congress.* They have nice incomes; they live in big houses; and *they owe us.*

So I'm saying that we find out, and publish, the names and addresses of ex-congresspersons—all those statespersons who, confronted with a temporary Social Security surplus, and knowing that a crunch was coming, shrewdly voted to invest billions in projects such as the B-2 "Stealth" Bomber (motto: "Ready to Defend America at Any Time! Unless It's Raining!").

Then, when we reach age 65, we would simply pack up our belongings and go to the home of a retired congressperson who resides in an area that we like. We'd ring the doorbell, and when the ex-congressperson answered, we'd say:

"Hi! You don't know me, but when you were in Congress, you voted to spend all of my future Social Security benefits on a Museum of Historic Cabbages in your home district, not to mention your own generous pension. So I'll be living in your guest bedroom, along with my Doberman pinscher, Buster. Hey! Looks like Buster wants to play with you! Ha ha! Usually those puncture wounds don't bleed for long. So, what's for lunch?"

Doesn't this sound like a fair solution to the Boomer retirement problem? Sure it does! The only potential flaw that I see is that the ex-congresspersons might not want us living with them. They might tell us to go away; they might even hire armed security guards. This is fine. Because if push comes to shove, the guards won't be shooting at us.

11
10 Signs That
You Might Be Losing It

1. You tend to forget things.

* * *

2. When you drive your car, you notice that people yell at you a lot. Often, these people are lying on your hood.

* * *

3. On more than one occasion, while shaving, you have noticed that your razor seemed kind of dull. Upon closer examination, your razor turned out to be your toothbrush.

* * *

4. You're always searching for the right word or name. You'll be telling an anecdote, and you'll get stuck on a name, and you'll tell your listeners: "You know! That guy! With the thing! He has that thing! That guy!" And everybody will start trying to guess who you're talking about, as if you're playing charades, and finally, after ten minutes of

this, it will turn out that the name you're trying to remember is: "The Pope." By this time, of course, you have no recollection of the original anecdote.

* * *

5. You sometimes address your spouse as "General Eisenhower."

* * *

6. You tend to forget things.

* * *

7. You sometimes wear a bathrobe to the office.

* * *

8. And it isn't your office.

* * *

9. It isn't your bathrobe, either.

* * *

10. You tend to forget things.

12
Confronting the Inevitability of Death

You Go Ahead. I'm Gonna Watch The Simpsons.

Death comes to all living things except crabgrass. We all know this, but most of us don't think about death much when we're young, because we're preoccupied with the concerns of youth, such as sex, and work, and having sex at work.

But when you turn 50, you find yourself thinking more about death, because more and more people your own age are—as William Shakespeare so poetically expressed it—"shuffling off this mortal coil and kicking the bucket." When you bump into people you haven't seen for a while, you find yourself having conversations like this:

OTHER PERSON: Did you hear about Bob Frumbish?
YOU: No! What happened?

OTHER PERSON: He died!

YOU: No!

OTHER PERSON: Yes!

YOU: That's *awful!*

OTHER PERSON: Yes! He took his grandson to a petting zoo, and he just keeled over! Onto a small goat! He was dead before he hit the ground!

YOU: The goat?

OTHER PERSON: No, Bob.

YOU: I can't believe it! *Bob Frumbish.*

OTHER PERSON: I know!

YOU (after thinking about it for a moment): Which one is Bob Frumbish again?

OTHER PERSON: You know! He's the one who . . . At least I *think* this was him . . . The one who, remember, he was in the Drama Club at Saint Emmet's, and during the rumble number in *West Side Story,* he was a Jet, and he threw up on one of the Sharks?

YOU: Saint Emmet's?

OTHER PERSON: You know . . . Saint Emmet's Academy for Unusually Sweaty Children. Didn't you go there?

YOU: No.

OTHER PERSON: Well, aren't you Norm . . . uh . . . Norm . . . Geez, I can't remember your last name.

YOU: Wirewhacker.

OTHER PERSON: No, that's not it.

YOU: No, I'm saying *my* last name is Wirewhacker. My name is Ted Wirewhacker.

OTHER PERSON: I don't know any Ted Wirewhacker . . . *Wait a minute.* If you're not Norm, how do you know Bob?
YOU: Bob who?

So we see that, when you pass 50, not only are your contemporaries dying, your brain cells are also dropping like flies. But my point is that you find yourself thinking more and more about the fact that one of these days your name[1] is going to be on the obituary pages. In fact, you have quietly started reading the obituary pages, and you find yourself scrutinizing them with an intensity that you formerly reserved for the sports pages. The difference is, you aren't checking to see if your favorite team won; you're checking to see how many of the people who died were younger than you. In fact, you wish the newspaper would save you the trouble of having to read a bunch of extraneous details about dead people you don't know, and instead just summarize the crucial information right on the front page of the newspaper, using a box-score format:

---

1. Probably spelled wrong.

PEOPLE YOUNGER THAN YOU
WHO DIED IN YOUR AREA YESTERDAY

Number of People	Cause of Death
8	Heart attack
5	Stroke
3	Auto accident
2	Failed to check shoes for scorpions
1	Routine dental checkup
14	Vegetarianism

With each passing year, we see more and more obituaries for people who were younger than we are. This makes many of us nervous, because we're not 100 percent sure what will happen to us after death.

One popular belief, of course, is that if we've been good, we go to Heaven and get to spend eternity with our dear departed Loved Ones. The problem with this is that we weren't exactly crazy about some of our Loved Ones before they departed. I mean, sure, we *loved* them, but they tended to drone on about non-compelling events that occurred in 1932, or act strange, or be less than diligent in the area of b.o. suppression. So, depending on the seating arrangements in Heaven, you could wind up spending all of eternity next to, say, Uncle Harley, who already ruined many of your childhood Thanksgiving meals by inserting his dentures at the table and smelling as though he was carrying around dead hamsters in his undershorts.

So Heaven doesn't sound like such a great post-life environment. On the other hand, you definitely don't want to go to Hell, and have to spend eternity with the likes of Hitler and Stalin and whoever invented telemarketing.

This brings us to another popular belief, held by practitioners of certain Eastern religions, as well as many highly influential and widely respected New Age wing nuts, which is that when you die, you get reincarnated and come back into this world in the form of another person or living thing.

I don't know about you, but I don't find the reincarnation scenario reassuring, either. I mean, it would be okay if you came back as some kind of creature that leads a fun and exciting life. My first choice would be to come back as a hornet. I would not be a hive-oriented type of hornet: I would be more of a freelance hornet, and I would spend most of my time in the U.S. House of Representatives, where I would buzz around menacingly and land on the noses of congresspersons giving speeches on C-Span, causing them to stop speaking and stare at me in cross-eyed terror. And when the other congresspersons said, "If you hold still, it won't sting you!"—I would respond, in a high-pitched but clearly audible voice:[2] "Like hell I won't!"

It goes without saying that I would also be a regular visitor to the home of Martha Stewart.

The problem is, there's no guarantee that you'll be reincarnated in the form of something as cool as a hornet. You could also come back as a totally wretched creature, such as a dung beetle or Mrs. Donald Trump.

---

2. I would be a talking hornet.

So I'm not thrilled about the possibility of reincarnation, either. Which leaves the third major possibility about death, which is that there's *nothing* afterward. That would mean that, as far as mortality is concerned, human beings are no different from cockroaches: One moment you're scurrying around on the kitchen floor of life, collecting the Cheez-It crumbs of daily existence; the next moment, you get stomped into bug glop by The Big Shoe from Above, and that's it, *finito,* you are nothing more than Purina-brand Bacteria Chow. This would mean that the sum total of your existence is the years you're now spending on earth. And when you get past 50, you begin having to deal with this concept:

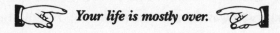 *Your life is mostly over.*

I mean, do the math! Let's say, for the sake of argument, that you expect to live to the ripe old age of 80. That *sounds* like a long time, until you realize that you've already lived 50 of those years, which means that, as a percentage of your total life, you have already lived . . . Let's see, divide 50 into . . . No, wait, divide 80 into . . .

Okay, let's just say that you have lived a healthy percentage of your life. There are definitely more years behind you than ahead. This can be depressing, especially if you have not achieved the goals that you set out for yourself in your youth. Perhaps you envisioned yourself one day running a large and successful corporation, and instead here you are, at age 50, working in a small, drafty cubicle and reporting to a 28-year-old Harvard MBA snot who never goes to lunch with you and keeps mispronouncing your name and takes two minutes to look at a project proposal that you've been working on for eight months, then bounces it back to you late on Friday afternoon with a big scrawled note across the cover saying, "TOO MANY SEMICOLONS."

And so, with a briefcase bulging with work to ruin your weekend, you trudge out to your car, which needs many repairs and has french-fries cartons under the front seat dating back to the Bush administration, but which you can't afford to replace because you're paying off the college loan you took out for your daughter, who has just informed you, in her senior year, that she has decided to drop out because she has met this really *wonderful*, really *spiritual* older man who calls himself "The One" and who has invited her to live with him and twenty-seven of his other followers in a communal yurt in northern Idaho until such time as the Mother Ship comes to take everybody back to the planet Krong. Just thinking about this makes you feel as though you have an irate wolverine trying to claw its way out of your stomach, which reminds you that your doctor is insisting that, because of these pains you've been having, you need to undergo an exploratory procedure in which you lie facedown and they insert about 130 feet of semi-flexible medical tubing into your body—"There will be some discomfort," your doctor says—and of course this procedure, which costs the equivalent of two weeks at a luxury resort in Tahiti, is not covered by your so-called medical plan, which as far as you can tell does not cover *any* medical procedure except possibly the Evil Spirits Cleansing Ritual, wherein primitive mud-smeared tribal individuals dance around you waving magic bones.

And so you think to yourself as you unlock your car, pull on the door handle, and watch it break off and fall into the parking-lot slush: *This was not the way things were supposed to turn out.* Fifty years! Most of your life gone! Time running out! The Big Shoe with your name on it hovering up there, somewhere! Is there *anything* you can do about this?

Yes, there is. You can take advantage of a brilliant accounting concept: *deductions.* Deductions are usually used in the area of income tax, to reduce a taxpayer's income. If a taxpayer has a gross income of, say, $185,000, he or she can reduce this by deducting legitimate expenses such as interest, charitable contributions, business-related travel, business-related meals, business-related motorboats, losing wagers on business-related racehorses, etc., so that this taxpayer ultimately winds up reporting a net taxable income of only $4,385.62. And all this is *perfectly legal,* provided that the taxpayer has full documentation and the Internal Revenue Service never actually looks at the tax return.

You can use this very same principle to prove that, even though you're 50, your life is not mostly over. You simply get out a piece of paper and add up all the time you spent in your younger years that turned out to be utterly wasted. For example:

- You can start with the first five years of your life, because you don't remember them anyway.
- You can add ages 12 through 18, because of zits.
- You can add all of college if you majored in English, psychology, sociology, philosophy, education, marketing, or anything involving the word "communications."

•You can add another 17 years, which represents the 148,920 hours you have spent watching television, with the only memorable piece of information you have gleaned in all that time being the fact that Rolaids consumes *up to 47 times its own weight* in excess stomach acid.

•You can add three years for the time you have spent sorting out and discarding, unopened, your third- and fourth-class mail.

•You can add two years for the amount of time you have spent on hold, and another six months for each effort you have made to speak to an actual human in "Customer Service."

•If you're a baseball fan, you can add the cumulative total of seven years you have spent watching the manager, the catcher, and the infielders scratch themselves while waiting for the relief pitcher to mosey out to the mound and start warming up.

•If you work for a large corporation, you can add the cumulative total of nine years you have spent reading status reports or business plans, or sitting in semi-darkened rooms listening to some charisma-impaired co-worker drone through a presentation of 832 incomprehensible color slides, every single one of which involves a "matrix."

. . . and so on. I'm sure you can think of many more ways in which you have flushed entire years of your life right down the Toilet of Time. Let's say, when you add them all up, you get a total of—I'll be conservative here—43 years. Think about that! *Forty-three years!* Forty-three precious, never-to-come-again years, completely wasted!

This is wonderful news. Because when you *deduct* these 43 wasted years from the 50 you have lived so far, you see that you've really lived for only . . . Let me just get out the old electronic calculator here . . . Okay, you've really lived for *only seven years!* You're a spring chicken! You have most of your life ahead of you, unless your stomach wolverine turns out to be serious!

So instead of thinking about death all the time, you need to start enjoying your life. The key here is to avoid repeating the mistakes you've made in the past. In other words: NO MORE WASTING TIME! And no more letting *others* waste your time, either. If you run into some acquaintance whom you have never really cared for, and this person suggests some kind of social get-together, *you must not waffle.* You must look this person directly in the eye and say: "I'm sorry, John, but my time is precious to me, and frankly I would rather have my appendix removed by baboons wielding unsterilized tuna-can lids than spend so much as five minutes listening to you and Elaine as you once again describe, item by item, in intricate detail, the late-night buffet on the cruise you took in 1983."

Likewise, at work, when the next endless slide presentation starts, you must not just sit there like the other corporate sheep. You must rise to your feet and ask: "Does anybody here actually know what a matrix *is*? And does anybody *give* a shit?" And then you must stride from the meeting room and back to your cubicle, where you must pick up the report that you were supposed to have reworked over the weekend, take it into the MBA snot's office, toss it into his lap, and say: "I figured out what you can do with the semicolons."

I'm not saying that this new, no-wasted-time philosophy will make your life perfect; what I'm saying is that at least you'll be *living*. True, you might soon be living in an appliance carton, but big deal! There's more to life than material comforts! Get off the damned money treadmill and experience the world around you! Stop to smell the roses; feel the sunshine; listen to the birds.

Do *not* mess with the hornets.

13
Conclusion

Looking Forward to a Brighter, Better Future. Or Whatever.

As I write these words, in the spring of 1998, it's a pretty good bet that, if you're part of the huge mass of people reaching 50, things have gone reasonably well for you. I'm not saying your life has been perfect. For example, your career probably did not turn out to be all you hoped for when you were young:

- **What you hoped your career would provide:** Excitement; creative challenge; financial reward; a chance to really "make a difference"; prestige, perhaps even a certain level of fame.
- **What you settled for:** A dental plan.

Still, most of us Baby Boomers have managed to hold down jobs and support ourselves, which is pretty impressive when you consider that when we started out, virtually all of our useful skills involved either Frisbees or cigarette papers. A lot of us also raised children, and although this did not turn out to be as simple as we thought—for example, we had NO idea how much assembly would be required—we managed to produce a generation of kids who will become solid, productive citizens once they gain a little maturity, remove their body piercings, start wearing normal-sized pants instead of what appear to be caterer's tents with pockets, and improve their academic performance to the point where they're competitive with, if not foreign kids, then at least the lower primates.

But for now, it's our generation that holds the reins of power. Bill Clinton, the quintessential Baby Boomer, is in the Oval Office, charting the course of world events. (Actually, as I write these words, Bill is meeting with his vast squadron of personal lawyers, trying to come up with a good explanation as to why at one point he had pretty much the entire federal government, including all major branches of the armed forces, trying to find a job for one intern. But once he's done with *that,* I'm sure he'll be back to charting the course of world events.)

Another Boomer, Bill Gates, is the most influential businessman on the planet, at the helm of an industry that has made it possible, via the almost-miraculous data-processing power of the computer microchip and the Internet, for almost any person, almost anywhere on the planet, to see Pamela Anderson naked.

Yes, we Boomers have made our mark on the modern world. Everywhere you look, you see Boomers running business; Boomers running government; Boomers running the TV networks; Boomers producing the movies; big, flabby, expanding Boomer butts squatting all over the cultural landscape. No *wonder* all the other generations hate us!

Tough noogies for them. This is our glory time, this last decade or so before our powers decline and we start showing up for work with our pants on backward. For now, we are the Big Dog of generations, the generation that will be in charge as we reach the year 2000 and celebrate the New Millennium. Already the excitement has started to build around this historic event, with millions of people making elaborate plans for December 31, 1999.[1] It's going to be the biggest celebration ever—the most anticipated, most discussed, most publicized single event in the history of human civilization. So it will definitely suck. It will be a grotesquely bloated version of every lame New Year's Eve party you ever went to, all those nights when you drank too much mediocre champagne and ended up wearing a stupid cardboard hat, blowing on a cheesy noisemaker, singing "Auld Lang Syne" (whatever *that* means) and thinking to yourself: "This is IT?"

The New Millennium stands to be a million times worse. Everybody will try desperately to make it Significant, but you just know that somehow, in the end, it will boil down to Dick Clark. If you have any sense whatsoever, you'll spend that night cleaning out your refrigerator.

But that is not my point. My point is that we Boomers are in our peak years of power and influence, and we need to start thinking about what kind of legacy we will leave for future gen-

---

1. Yes, I know there are people who argue that the New Millennium actually doesn't begin until a year later, at midnight on December 31, 2000. And what is more, I don't care.

erations. What will our grandchildren say about us? Will they say that we were responsible caretakers of the planet that we led into the twenty-first century? Or will they say that we squandered the precious gifts that were entrusted to us?

Who cares what they say? As I noted in the Introduction, we'll be dead. If natural causes don't get us, the Asteroid of Doom will. You've read about this: According to scientists, there's a large asteroid—I'm talking about an asteroid nearly *twice* the size of Shaquille O'Neal—hurtling through space on a trajectory that may, in the year 2028, cause it to crash into Earth, a disastrous occurrence that could result in cataclysmic physical damage, severe long-term changes in the weather, the potential destruction of human civilization, and what the International Committee of Alarmed Astrophysicists has described as "potentially the biggest class-action lawsuit ever filed."

So maybe we don't need to be so worried about our legacy. Maybe, when our grandchildren come around and sit on our knee and look up at us with big innocent eyes and ask, "Grandma or Grandpa, when I grow up, will there be clean water for me to drink and clean air for me to breathe and a strong economy and world peace?" we will be able to just chuckle in a grandparently way and answer: "There's no need to worry about that, little Johnny! The Asteroid of Doom will probably squash us like seedless grapes under a sledgehammer!"

And the grandchild will say: "My name isn't Johnny."

And we'll say: "Well, then, get off my knee."

Acknowledgments

I want to start by thanking Rita Lang Kleinfelder, who researched and wrote a fascinating book called *When We Were Young: A Baby-Boomer Yearbook* (760 pp., illus.), which provided much of the information I used in this book for the chapters on the early Boomer years. Most of the actual facts in those chapters came from Rita's book; any errors came from me.

I also thank my editor at Crown, Betty Prashker, for always being cheerful and supportive and never coming right out and saying that the manuscript is approximately a decade overdue. I thank my agent, Al Hart, who was a Baby Boomer *way* before anybody else had even thought about it.

I thank my wife, Michelle, who always insists that I am young, and my son, Rob, who provides perspective by insisting that I am incredibly old. Above all, I thank my parents, Dave and Marion, for deciding to go ahead and have me at such an amazingly interesting time.

About the Author

DAVE BARRY is a Pulitzer prize-winning columnist and the bestselling author of *Dave Barry Is from Mars and Venus, Dave Barry in Cyberspace, Dave Barry's Guide to Guys,* and other books. He lives in Miami, Florida, of course.

DAVE BARRY IN CYBERSPACE

A self-professed computer geek who actually does Windows,
Dave Barry takes us on a hilarious hard drive via the
information superhighway—and into the very heart of
cyberspace. Inside you'll find juicy bytes on:

- How to Buy and Set Up a Computer; Step One: Get Valium
- Nerdstock in the Desert; Or: Bill Gates Is Elvis
- Software: Making Your Computer Come Alive
So It Can Attack You
- Word Processing: How to Press
an Enormous Number of Keys
Without Ever Actually Writing Anything
- Selected Web Sites, including Cursing in Swedish,
Deformed Frog Pictures, and
The Toilets of Melbourne, Australia

"RELENTLESSLY FUNNY."
—PEOPLE

"SIDE-SPLITTING."
—ST. PETERSBURG TIMES

Available in bookstores everywhere
Published by Ballantine Books
The Random House Publishing Group
www.ballantinebooks.com

DAVE BARRY DOES JAPAN

It introduced him to a mouth-watering array of Far Eastern culinary delights ("the Japanese routinely eat things that have eyeballs or suckers or other flagrantly unacceptable organs still attached to them") and exposed him to high culture ("one hour of watching Kabuki is the equivalent of seventeen hours spent in a more enjoyable activity, such as eye surgery"). Join Dave Barry as he explores culture shock in all its numerous, humorous forms, including:

- Failing to Learn Japanese in Only Five Minutes
  (Or: "Very Much Good Morning, Sir!")
- Secrets of Japanese Industry
  (I Probably Should Have Written Them Down)
- Humor in Japan (Take My Tofu! Please!)
- Sports in Japan ("Yo, Batter! Loudly Make It Fly!")
- Staying at a Japanese Inn (Peace, Tranquillity, Insects)

"ON TARGET . . .
A RARE AND SPECIAL TREAT."
—THE NEW YORK TIMES BOOK REVIEW

Available in bookstores everywhere
Published by Ballantine Books
The Random House Publishing Group
www.ballantinebooks.com

DAVE BARRY'S GUIDE TO GUYS

If you're a guy—or if you're attempting to share a remote control with one—you need this book, because in it Dave Barry deals frankly and semi-thoroughly with such important guy issues as:

- Scratching
- The role of guys in world history, including the heretofore-unknown relationship between the discovery of North America and golf
- Why the average guy can remember who won the 1960 World Series, but not necessarily the names of all his children
- Why guys cannot simultaneously think and look at breasts
- Secret guy orgasm-delaying techniques, including the Margaret Thatcher Method

"AN AVERAGE OF THREE TO FOUR LAUGHS PER PAGE . . . DAVE BARRY IS ONE FUNNY HUMAN."
—SAN FRANCISCO EXAMINER

"Whether you're a guy—or attempting to share a bathroom with one—Barry has some wacky words of wisdom for you."
—USA TODAY

Available in bookstores everywhere
Published by Ballantine Books
The Random House Publishing Group
www.ballantinebooks.com